S0-BCR-083

971.404
BER

Bertrand, Guy,

Enough is enough :
an attorney's
struggle for
democracy in

ENOUGH IS ENOUGH

An Attorney's Struggle for Democracy in Quebec

Guy BERTRAND

Written in collaboration with Angéline Fournier
Translated by Marie Thérèse Blanc

ECW PRESS

Copyright © ECW PRESS, 1996

All rights reserved. No part of this publication may be reproduced, stored in a retrieval system, or transmitted in any form by any process — electronic, mechanical, photocopying, recording, or otherwise — without the prior written permission of ECW PRESS.

CANADIAN CATALOGUING IN PUBLICATION DATA

Bertrand, Guy, 1937–
Enough is enough

Translation of: Plaidoyer pour les citoyens.

ISBN 1-55022-302-X

1. Bertrand, Guy, 1937–   . 2. Referendum – Quebec (Province). 3. Citizens for a Democratic Nation (Organization). 4. Quebec (Province) – History – Autonomy and independence movements.
5. Canada – Constitutional law.
I. Fournier, Angéline.   II. Title.

FC2925.9.R4B4713 1996 971.4´04 C96-931218-0
F1053.2.B4713 1996

The English translation of this book was made possible through the Translation Grants Program of The Canada Council. The author and publisher are grateful for the Council's support.

Design and imaging by ECW Type & Art, Oakville, Ontario.
Printed by Imprimerie Gagné Ltée, Louiseville, Québec.

Distributed in Canada by General Distribution Services, 30 Lesmill Road, Don Mills, Ontario M3B 2T6.

Distributed in the United States by Login Publishers Consortium, 1436 West Randolph Street, Chicago, Illinois, U.S.A. 60607.

Published by ECW PRESS,
2120 Queen Street East, Suite 200,
Toronto, Ontario M4E 1E2.

"We cannot spend our entire
lives trying to separate;
in the end we must
learn to live together."

To Lisette, my wife, who always stood
by my side when I spoke throughout
Quebec in favour of independence, yet
who was also the first to impress upon
me that we cannot spend our lives,
as a people, trying to separate.

To my children, Johanne, Jean-François,
Marie-France, and Dominique, who, along
with their mother, never hesitated to support
me at this turning point in my life.

To Stéphanie, my granddaughter, who as
an adult, will, I hope, be a witness to a
modern Quebec capable of living with
Canada in a state of perfect harmony.

TABLE OF CONTENTS

Introduction 9

1. The Choice Facing Quebeckers 13
2. Our Very Own Armchair Revolutionaries . . 42
3. The Coup d'État 67
4. Renouncing Independence 112
5. Learning to Live Together 129

Guy Bertrand v. The Honorable Paul
   Bégin et al.: The Judgement of the
   Honorable Robert Lesage, J.S.C. 149

Introduction

I DEDICATE THIS book to those who believe in Canada, as I do to those who believe in Quebec independence, who hesitate, who have made up their minds, or who think that the time has come to reflect upon a debate that has been tearing apart our society for over twenty years.

I dedicate this book to those ordinary citizens who have become, much against their will, hostages to an élite of dogmatic separatists, who will not hesitate to deceive the people in order to achieve their goal: the separation of Quebec. No thought is given to the ominous consequences of this choice for the rest of the population as this élite goes on manipulating information, planning strategy, putting forward unrealistic partnership deals, and favouring an outdated option that represents a step backwards for Quebec and Canada as a whole.

I fought, throughout my professional life, for those who needed a voice in the struggle against governmental and institutional abuses. I have, since my youth, taken sides in a determined, political manner in favour of the Quebec people, the unemployed, welfare recipients, and all those with neither the means nor the will to defend themselves. Even in my days as a hard-line separatist, I always defended the cause of democracy.

As I undertook to question my own views, I became perfectly aware that I was cutting myself off from some of my friends and part of my family. I knew that I would never be forgiven for leaving the ranks of the Parti Québécois.

Yet I knew, too, that we were all responsible for telling the truth to the people of Quebec, from whom nothing must be withheld, who must be made aware of the disastrous socioeconomic consequences of Quebec separation, and who are mature enough to make an informed decision about their options.

If I have changed gears recently, it is because I am certain that the separatist cause, in 1996, is but a vestige of an outdated and now groundless debate that stands in the way of Quebec's progress and of its getting ready to take up the challenges posed by the twenty-first century.

Worse yet, the Parti Québécois government, led by Jacques Parizeau and supported by Lucien Bouchard, plotted, in 1995, a constitutional coup d'état in the form of a unilateral secession that would have driven all of Quebec society into a serious crisis. Thus I chose to bring part of my struggle before the courts in order to challenge our separatist leaders, who had knowingly decided to flout democracy and the fundamental principle of the rule of law, according to which Quebec separation requires the consent of the partners involved, and a negotiated amendment to the Canadian constitution.

I could have kept quiet. Given the seriousness of the situation, I decided to speak out and hoped by the same token to persuade a number of separatists to reexamine their positions. I chose, as I always did when I belonged to the Parti Québécois, to engage in battle openly, frankly, and responsibly, for in matters of politics, the dissemination of information is the best way of protecting citizens' rights.

In this book, I try to share with Quebeckers the reasons that have led me, once and for all, to say NO to the separatist project. I try as well to inform them of the harmful social and economic consequences of separation for Quebec, and to warn them of the dangers of unilateral secession.

My message is aimed also at the separatist élite, who must concede that they have failed. Twice, in 1980 and 1995, Quebeckers said NO to separation from Canada. Meanwhile, all polls indicate that the separatist option stagnates at around 30 percent of voter support. This élite must put an end to its abuse of our democratic system and stop devising elaborate strategies to draw an extra 21 percent of the population into voting unwillingly for an unwanted independence.

In the following chapters I hope, finally, to encourage Quebeckers to let bygones be bygones and to recognize that being a part of Canada represents our best chance of success.

I do not, however, claim to exhaust the subject, and neither do I take a stand on matters relating to the renewal of federalism or to decentralization. Important as it may be for our political élite, this debate is not that of the people. Above all, this same élite must stop sitting on the fence, the threat of independence on one side to be used as a negotiation tool, and, on the other, only a half-hearted adherence to Canada.

Canadian federalism is, in fact, synonymous with success. We have managed to develop the distinct nature of our identity within Canada, and we may develop it further. In order to flourish, however, we must embrace success without reservation.

I am not certain that the political élite of Quebec can completely reverse its thinking on these issues. I therefore address myself directly to the people, so that they may draw their own conclusions.

I pray that my self-examination sheds some light on the outdated and destructive goals of separation, and that it may convince Quebeckers that the time has come to close a chapter and move on.

Changes will occur if we work together towards greater openness to the rest of the world and cease trying to cut ourselves off from each other. We must forsake past quarrels and look upon the future in a new and positive way in order to create the better society about which we all dream. Only then will we finally regain, along with subsequent generations, our trust in the future.

The Canada we have built together represents part of the heritage of all Quebeckers; it is our duty to make it thrive so that we may pass along to our children a prosperous and united country.

CHAPTER ONE

The Choice Facing Quebeckers

QUEBEC IS AT a crossroads. The choice is ours: we may turn this land into a modern state that faces the future from within Canada, or into a state withdrawn into itself, torn by incessant quarrels, and undermined by an ethnocentric and self-centred nationalism that keeps us from acknowledging that the world has changed. By renouncing the separatist option, I choose to contribute to the founding of this modern state within Canada.

We Cannot Spend Our Lives Trying to Separate . . .

Many have asked me to explain my change of heart. I was a Parti Québécois militant for twenty-five years; in fact, I helped found the party, alongside René Lévesque. I worked day and night to promote the Quebec separatist project. I led the battle within the party against its most moderate members.

In 1985, following René Lévesque's departure, I stood for the presidency of the Parti Québécois. In 1989, at the request of Jacques Parizeau, who came to Quebec City on three occasions to win me over to the idea, I became a party candidate for the Louis-Hébert riding. I was on friendly terms with Parizeau and he suggested that I present myself once again in the 1994 election. I declined the offer. I was already on the path that would lead to my rejection of the separatist cause.

I slowly began to understand that we had failed, that the majority of the population did not wish to separate from Canada, and that the debate on this issue was dividing our society and blocking its way to progress.

We had obtained from Canada what we needed in order to ensure Quebec's development, but we no longer knew where to stop. We no longer knew how to tell ourselves or the party's militant wing that enough was enough.

The party had become accustomed to always asking for more; the separatist wheel had turned into an engine that generated propaganda and produced crisis after crisis. I saw it poisoning our public life, dividing our families and friends, destroying the social fabric, and causing citizens to flee. I saw Quebec becoming poorer, Montreal declining, and everything that we had built together crumble into dust. I saw the energy being wasted and funds being squandered in discussions that divided us a little further each time. These reasons and many others led me to reconsider my separatist convictions.

I left the Parti Québécois, for I no longer wished to participate in what had become an enormous swindle. The separatist élite, to achieve its aims at whatever cost, no longer hesitated to fool the population and hide from it the true consequences of Quebec separation.

I am of the opinion that we must take note of our accomplishments and turn over a new leaf before it is too late. Canada belongs to us; she is our strongest ally.

Because I had always defended the interests of citizens against institutional abuses, I did not hesitate to challenge

my own beliefs. I invite all sincere separatists and national-
ists to do the same.

I broadened my horizons, and opened my eyes and my
mind. I listened to the other side. I read on the subjects of
federalism and Canadian history. Finally, I came to the
conclusion that, after twenty-five years, it was time for me
to revise my thinking!

I readily admit that it is never easy to reconsider one's
convictions. There were difficult times, yet I regret nothing:
neither those initial moments, nor those that followed. I
discovered, instead, a Quebec and a Canada I hardly knew,
and many Quebeckers have since told me that they have
travelled a similar road.

My change of direction occurred gradually. Throughout
this work, I shall present as questions the arguments that
persuaded me to modify my opinions. I present here the
chronology of events that led me to rethink my original
choice.

For several years, I had been questioning our need for
independence on the eve of the twenty-first century, the role
played by nation-states, our stake in Canada, and the
workings of federalism. I began doubting my own position,
for I recognized that Quebec was becoming sovereign from
within Canada, which is to say that it was developing its
ability to grow in accordance with its needs.

Why separate in a world in which nation-states are outdated, when today's states attempt to work together and
form solid alliances? Was Canada not offering us a type of
federal arrangement much better suited to the requirements of our world? Did the flexibility of federalism not
allow us to attain, in a progressive manner, the changes we
required?

These thoughts had begun to unsettle my convictions. I
realized that the world, Canada, and Quebec were evolving,
but that the separatist élite refused to react accordingly.

We were using, in the 1990s, the same arguments that I had elaborated upon in my writings from the late 1970s!

Quebeckers were not fooled: only 20 to 30 percent desired independence. I therefore asked myself the following questions: How could it be that we were unable to sway an important majority of Quebeckers in favour of independence when, for twenty-five years, we had spared no effort in that direction? Could it be that we were on the wrong path? Could it be that our adherence to Canada is, in fact, a more viable option for Quebec?

I wished to spend the best years of my life in harmony; in a quest for a better understanding of my fellow Quebeckers, be they francophone, anglophone, allophone, or aboriginal. I wished to devote myself to a constructive and unifying scheme, something that the independence project could not claim to be.

A series of events nonetheless proved decisive.

I began to distance myself from the Parti Québécois around 1992, when I saw that it no longer allowed for dissent. I have, indeed, always insisted on the respect of democratic principles. When Bill 101 had the effect of suspending the use of English on bilingual signs, thus curtailing the freedom of expression of the anglophone minority, I opposed the *Péquiste* élite and supported the 1993 proposal put forward by Claude Ryan, who suggested, in compliance with the Supreme Court ruling on the matter, that signs include more than one language.

So long as the French language is given prominence on commercial signs — for we are on French territory — we, the members of a civilized society, have no right to keep citizens from posting signs in an additional language. Thus if anglophone or allophone Quebeckers wish to welcome their customers with signs written also in English, Chinese, Italian, or Greek, who can prevent them from doing so? The francophones, because they make up the majority of the Quebec population? The argument is defective. All citizens are equal; we enjoy the same rights and are bound by the same obligations. We may all speak our mother tongue so long as we respect the language of the majority.

The Supreme Court has, moreover, clearly stated that the prohibition of the use, on commercial signs, of any language other than French constitutes a breach of freedom of expression as guaranteed by the Canadian Charter of Rights and Freedoms. Thus the Court nullified certain of Bill 101's provisions concerning such signs. The Court further held that the Quebec government could protect and promote the French language by requiring that business owners give priority to French messages while allowing them at the same time to use other languages.

A Parti Québécois poll, taken at that time, indicated that 65 percent of the *Péquistes* were willing to live with bilingual and even trilingual signs. The party élite, however, was opposed to the idea. This particular debate revealed to me the intolerance that prevailed in those circles.

Then came the 1993 election to parliament of the Bloc Québécois. "Enough!" I remember telling myself. "We cannot spend our entire lives trying to separate; in the end we must learn to live together." Were we not in the process of taking advantage of Canadian democracy? Would any other country have embraced, as her official opposition, a party dedicated to national destruction? Some time later, Lucien Bouchard narrowly escaped death and we were all affected by this turn of events. I wrote him a letter wishing him a speedy recovery, and he wrote back. I knew him well. We had talked over the matter of his departure from the Conservative Party and he had, on one occasion, even come over for dinner.

I was extremely moved by the outpouring of sympathy that rushed in from Canada when Lucien Bouchard became ill. Canadians from all over the country and deputies from all political parties sincerely hoped that the Bloc Québécois leader would recover. Some cried, others were upset, and all seemed deeply saddened by the news. Something occurred to me then: though we had spared no effort to destroy Canada in the past two decades, we remained part of the Canadian family.

In 1994, the Parti Québécois came to power. Its leader, Jacques Parizeau, was determined to obtain Quebec independence at all costs.

In December 1994, the Parizeau government sent every home a copy of the draft sovereignty bill. Clearly all energies would be devoted to obtaining a YES majority at the next referendum.

Yet all studies indicated that the cost of independence was likely to be exorbitant! We had no right to drag the population into an adventure that threatened to amount to collective suicide. We had, at the very least, a duty to inform the people of Quebec of the risks involved. The independence project no longer led to self-determination. It led, instead, to the self-destruction of Quebec.

Who would be left holding the baby after separation? Middle-class Quebeckers without opportunities elsewhere, millions of unemployed citizens, welfare recipients, young people, and the elderly. All those, in short, without the means to defend themselves or to come through what promised to become a veritable economic disaster and, most probably, a social catastrophe as well.

When I was still a member of the Parti Québécois, we would shrug off all matters related to the economy. I write about this further on. "Numbers!" we would say. "Numbers are immaterial. What counts is that we have guts!" But we knew our own weaknesses and, whether we admitted it or not, we knew that sooner or later we would bear a hefty bill.

I nonetheless considered it my duty to ask myself what my share of the blame would be if, as a separatist, I threw my support behind a cause that drastically lowered Quebeckers' standard of living and might ultimately degenerate into violent, ethnic infighting. I discovered that a separate Quebec offered its citizens no guarantee of prosperity or social stability.

Worse yet, the Parti Québécois government, led by Jacques Parizeau and supported by Lucien Bouchard, plotted, as early as 1994, a constitutional coup d'état in the form of a unilateral secession that would have driven all of Quebec society into a serious crisis. The draft sovereignty bill, of which we all owned a copy, was extremely clear on this subject.

Given the gravity of this state of affairs, I did not hesitate to testify publicly at a hearing held in Quebec City on February 15, 1995 by the Commission on the Future of Quebec. Even with the support of my family, this proved difficult. I stood before a separatist audience, some members of which I had personally brought into the party.

I showed up with a written text, but hoped that I would not have to read it. What I had to say was so painful that I wondered how I would be able to speak out in public. I wanted to tell my friends that, despite the twenty-five years I had spent by their side fighting a strenuous battle, I could suddenly go no further. I wanted to tell them that I may have taken a wrong turn, and that a YES victory would certainly hurl Quebec into a crisis from which it would never recover.

The room was filled to capacity; many had come to hear what I had to say. I was given a rather unfriendly reception. "Are you crazy?" one of my Parti Québécois friends asked me, looking visibly shaken. "Get a grip on yourself, pal!" Clearly my doubts seemed preposterous to him. I was deeply moved when I finally delivered my speech:

All the men and women of Quebec know, in their heart of hearts, that Quebec and Canada have grown prosperous together, and that the success of each can be attributed to the other's cooperation and collaboration. Canadians from the rest of Canada are our best friends, our best allies, and our best partners. . . . The Parti Québécois' approach to the referendum, clever as it may be, ought to be cast aside, for it is being dictated to Quebeckers, it is dividing the population, it is worse than the *status quo*, and it is suicidal.

I tried to explain that the separatist scheme was, from a juridical standpoint, hardly workable; someone would end up challenging it in court.

I added that the division of the Canadian national debt would lead to the collapse of Quebec's public finances. Even the economists most sympathetic to the sovereignist cause, such as Pierre Fortin, were predicting that the incidental costs of independence would be steep. I ended my speech by asking the government to give up on the idea of holding a referendum on the future of Quebec unless it could formulate a plan likely to win over a significant portion of the population.

I was extremely worried about the future of Quebeckers, for I feared social and economic upheavals. This time, perhaps, all the subterfuge devised by the Quebec government would ensure a majority of 50 percent plus 1. Even with such a narrow majority, the government would press on with its secessionist plan.

My testimony before the Commission was meant as an appeal to my separatist friends to reconsider their position. I meant, as well, to sound the alarm to warn the people of Quebec of the dangers ahead.

I was heckled during my speech and, as I left the room, I was insulted and compared to Lord Durham, but I chalked those words up to anger.

In the spring of 1995, the commissioners submitted their

reports, and Lucien Bouchard, Jacques Parizeau, and Mario Dumont, the leaders of three of Quebec's political parties, signed a "partnership" agreement that they claimed to want to put forward to the rest of Canada. Thus they hoped to win the referendum by deceiving the population. Opinion polls, however, continued to indicate that the people of Quebec were opposed to separation.

The Parti Québécois government was determined to act illegally and to show nothing but contempt for the Canadian constitution. This was totally unacceptable.

In July 1995, I asked Jacques Parizeau one last time to revise his strategy. I then chose to bring part of my struggle, on behalf of Quebeckers and against our separatist leaders, before the courts. These same leaders had knowingly decided to flout democracy and the Canadian constitution, according to which Quebec separation requires the consent of the partners involved as well as a negotiated constitutional amendment.

I have, since then, never ceased to expose the fraudulent misrepresentations that shroud the separatist project, just as I have never stopped battling the separatist élite that does severe damage to the people's cause.

Why and at What Cost Independence?

In the past, Quebeckers were told that they must choose between independence and integration. The latter meant that sooner or later the people of Quebec would lose themselves in the Canadian federation. Twenty years ago, our motivation was our desire to live, fully and completely, as francophones on this parcel of land on the North American continent. Like many of my friends, I believed that we did not stand a ghost of a chance to protect our identity, our culture, our distinctiveness, or our language without becoming a sovereign state.

The times have changed, however. Despite desperate rumours to the contrary, the French language has never been stronger in Quebec. Though it is true that we often feel that our mother tongue and culture are under siege in a continent in which the dominant language is English, we must face up to reality.

Canada hardly stifled our francophone identity; we were, instead, left to thrive as we spoke our mother tongue. Regardless of what some may say, Canada has recognized in our distinctiveness a facet of the Canadian identity as a whole.

Why, then, invoke the same ghosts at every available opportunity and insist on a form of independence that might compromise our cultural, economic, and social achievements?

In Praise of Canadian Democracy

Democracy forms the basis of any stable, prosperous, and cohesive society. Can a separate Quebec offer us a type of democracy that would be an improvement over the one we already know? Canadian democracy is renowned the world over and, given our political élite, I am unconvinced that we could do better on our own.

These past thirty years, separatists have done everything in their power to attack and destroy Canada, and I participated in these schemes. We must acknowledge, however, that it was thanks to the strength and flexibility of Canadian democracy that we were left undisturbed and free to act in this manner.

With our speeches and writings, we have systematically sought to demolish Canada, and to humiliate both its leaders and those francophone Quebeckers who chose to work on the federalist scene. We attacked them harshly and viciously; we accused them of being traitors and of being responsible for all our misfortunes.

We have taught our men and women that Quebec, and not Canada, is their true country, and now some are embarrassed to admit that they are proud to be Canadian. We also boycotted all Canadian symbols. It is quite out of the question for us to honour the Canadian flag — or the "red maple," as many separatists still like to call it. Let's not even mention the Canadian national anthem. During hockey matches at the Montreal Forum or at the Quebec Coliseum, we asked the public to remain seated and refrain from singing *Ô Canada*. Our flag was the *"fleurdelisé"* and *Gens du pays* was practically our anthem. Union leaders and separatist politicians tried, by every means possible, to ruin Quebeckers' natural fondness for Canada. Numerous songwriters, artists, philosophers, and poets contributed actively to this endeavour. No effort was spared; no stone was left unturned.

We were not, however, content to speak out and write against Canada. In 1968, we founded the Parti Québécois, which, at the same time as it claimed to work for the creation of a nation, deliberately sought the destruction of Canada.

In 1980, the Parti Québécois government launched the first referendum on sovereignty-association. This referendum was of a consultative nature and was therefore democratic, yet throughout the preceding months and during the referendum campaign itself the separatist cause was given a strong push.

Later we established the Bloc Québécois, a party also entirely devoted to the destruction of Canada as we know it. In 1993, we elected a majority of separatist delegates to represent Quebec on Parliament Hill. Led by Lucien Bouchard, an ex-federal Cabinet minister and former Canadian ambassador, the Bloc Québécois formed the official federal opposition party.

Would any other nation allow for the existence of a political movement that systematically threatens the integrity of the state and disrupts national unity? Would any other country accept, as the government's official opposition, a party that does not protect the interests of the nation as requested by its mandate, but seeks, day in and day out, to sabotage our political machine in order to destabilize the federation?

In 1994, we again elected to power the Parti Québécois, which had grown more separatist than ever. This time, the party was led by Jacques Parizeau.

In 1995, the Parti Québécois government launched a second referendum, which, far from being of a consultative nature, was meant instead to lead to an immediate and unilateral secession from Canada.

The Canadian government never tried to keep us from devising our separatist strategies. Rather than using force, Canada opted for a rational and conciliatory approach.

The government of any other country would have resorted to its own version of the War Measures Act, or would have taken similar steps to protect peace, order, and good government. Thanks to the democratic institutions that they paradoxically try to destroy, this country's separatists have, on the contrary, been blessed with the opportunity to promote their cause in every possible way. Yet despite an insidious referendum question and a systematic disinformation campaign on the part of the provincial government, the separatist project was once again rejected in 1995.

We must face reality: all separatist efforts notwithstanding, the nation bends, but does not break. To this day, few Quebeckers want a divided country.

Canada is a model of democracy; our duty as her citizens is to protect our democratic institutions. Canada is not the enemy. Canada and Quebec are each other's best allies, and they need each other to grow.

The Narrow and Egocentric Nature of French Nationalism

While Canada, Quebec, and the rest of the world moved on, separatists remained fixated on a type of rhetoric adopted a quarter of a century ago. We must not be afraid of change. Avoidable difficulties and clashes occur when, despite the planet's evolution, people remain entrenched in their old habits and thought processes.

Yes, the world has changed. The planet is now much smaller, and the problems we encounter become increasingly complex as the stakes involved assume global proportions. Thus pollution crosses all borders, the depletion of the ozone layer has planetary consequences, and geopolitical security is a world-wide concern. Because it is so intimately linked with today's information age (telecommunications, transportation, and so on), globalization is picking up speed. Travellers may cross the world in 24 hours. Television viewers in different countries end up watching the same programmes. Governments attempt to ward off the destabilizing effect of thousands of billions of dollars transferred every day by international investors on the information highway.

The gap between rich and poor keeps widening. According to Ricardo Petrella, President of the Lisbon Club, the poorest 10 percent of the population are twice as poor as they were in 1960, and the wealthiest are twice as wealthy. Though the world generates five times more resources than it did in 1960, our capacity to redistribute these riches has deteriorated.

Unemployment, which has reached unprecedented levels, is the bane of all industrialized countries. Among OECD (Organization for Economic Cooperation and Development) nations, unemployment has risen from 3.1 percent in the 1970s to 10 percent in 1993, leaving 35 million people without jobs. These figures exclude other inactive persons, such as those discouraged workers who fail to register with an unemployment office, or unwilling part-time workers.

Today's nations attempt to coordinate their efforts in order to solve their problems jointly. In these days when we must pool our resources and work towards better social and economic conditions, fruitless debates and old constitutional quarrels need to be cast aside.

Instead of opening up to the world, we keep retreating to a form of nationalism that has become self-centred, selfish, and, within certain circles, even slightly fanatical.

Given the above global trends, the Quebec government's desire to separate, on the grounds that it cannot agree with Ottawa on minor administrative details relating, for instance, to control over job training, is clearly anomalous. Meanwhile, each year, throughout the world, millions perish from hunger or in ethnic clashes.

Who, in Quebec, cares about any of this? We find our problems, our flag, our culture, our business, and our egos so much more engaging. Are we not, after all, the very centre of the universe?

This form of nationalism is dangerous. It is fanned by separatists. It carries within itself the seeds of discord, animosity, hatred, frustration, and anger. In Quebec, a nationalism of this kind might give rise to defiance and lead to hostilities.

A Cause That Is Not the People's Cause

We are clearly faced with a phenomenon brought about by a controlling bourgeois élite, the members of which have managed, through their intelligence, their knowledge, and their persuasiveness, to lead a large portion of the population to believe that separation is imperative when, in fact, the majority of the people is opposed to the idea.

Have we ever been witness, in Quebec, to a group of five hundred or a thousand persons marching through the streets or standing before Parliament, clamouring for independence? This *never* happens! Of course, we do hear cries of *"le Québec aux Québécois!"* but only during Saint Jean-Baptiste celebrations or Parti Québécois rallies.

Most Quebeckers no longer want independence, yet the élite keeps trying to force it upon them by repeating, again and again, that Canada represents an unworkable option.

Canada will, in fact, continue to thrive, especially if we work to improve it. Unfortunately, few Quebec federalists have the courage to admit, and to assert in a compelling manner, that they are opposed to independence.

Certain members of the Quebec élite and of the intellectual bourgeoisie, and some university professors, union leaders, and members of the press, seem to revel in their own pessimism. Journalists, in particular, are largely responsible for the morose climate we encounter these days at the heart of Quebec society. They seem more interested in covering instances of discord than they are in the solutions to our existing problems. To our newspeople, constant activity and political quarrels are the stuff that scoops and news are made of.

We must ask ourselves what would happen if, instead of covering the usual bickering between politicians, reporters were to convey, in an objective manner, messages to the effect that Canada is not the prison that has been described to us, and that Canadians actually live in harmony. Citizens would doubtless hold up their heads again. Rather than giving in to despair — an understandable reaction given the circumstances — they would realize that together they can accomplish much. Before this happens, of course, reporters will have to understand that our constitutional quarrels, though they have helped sell newspapers for decades, are of no interest to the people of Quebec.

The Parti Québécois must, in turn, stop looking after its own interests, which it has consistently done in the past, and start acting for the common good of the people. Party members, if they had their hearts set on ensuring Quebeckers' welfare, would do everything in their power to arrive at a popular consensus about a collective cause. This could only happen if the party renounced part of its nationalist aspirations and began focusing on the people, who can no longer bear to hear about independence. Unfortunately, at this point in time, a change of direction on the part of our leaders seems highly unlikely.

To Be or Not To Be Modern

Do we want to live in a shrivelled, embittered Quebec or in a modern Quebec, boldly facing the future, and at peace with the old separatist ghosts? As long as we hesitate to choose the latter we shall remain helpless witnesses to the gradual and inevitable weakening of Quebec.

We may, however, choose to relinquish our outdated hopes and opt instead for the greater social and economic welfare that may be obtained by way of our full participation in the Canadian federation.

We must, unequivocally, favour Canada and renounce separation, and we must all work together. Only then will we be able to pursue our growth and turn Quebec into a prosperous state — perhaps even the most dynamic and vigorous of states — within North America.

Because of her membership in the Canadian economic union, Quebec enjoys many benefits, such as access to the

Atlantic and Europe. The seaway, in turn, provides a passage to the United States by way of the Great Lakes.

Quebec's air, rail, and highway corridors lead to the vast and dynamic markets of the eastern and northeastern parts of the United States nearby. New England is at our doorstep. Within about 500 miles we hit the urban passage that stretches from Boston to Washington, D.C., and includes New York, Baltimore, Philadelphia, and Pittsburgh. A little farther, in the northern mideast, we have the states of Ohio, Michigan, Wisconsin, Illinois, and Indiana.

Three hundred miles to the south of Montreal, the state of New York affords us with a consumer market that exceeds that of Canada as a whole. Eight hundred miles from here, the Chicago-Boston-Washington triangle provides a market of over 100 million inhabitants. It is up to us to seize these opportunities and those offered as well by Canadian markets.

There is no doubt that we could turn Quebec into a modern, prosperous state within Canada. As such, we would be the envy of the world.

Quebec also enjoys the benefits of two spoken languages. Europeans feel right at home here, for we are, after all, francophone North Americans. We differ from those who speak French in Belgium, France, or Switzerland, for our lifestyle is distinctively American. Consequently, those Europeans who wish to settle in the northern half of our continent would likely settle in Quebec first.

Furthermore, our ability to speak English makes us comfortable dealing with Canadian or American markets. As full members of the Canadian federation, we may confidently take up any challenge.

You will tell me that we are presently doing just that. Quebec has, indeed, grown a great deal in the past twenty years. Yet we can only go further if we decide that we no longer wish to fall back upon ourselves. We must therefore clearly ask our leaders to forsake their separatist project and choose the future over an outdated cause.

It is now up to the people of Quebec to mobilize and tell their political leaders, in no uncertain terms, that they can no longer bear to live in a constant state of uncertainty. Even the mere threat of secession causes us to regress. It scares away investors, capital, commercial enterprises, and some of the most talented people in various fields.

Quebec's socio-economic situation is calamitous. There are 815,000 people on welfare, and about 400,000 people unemployed. In short, about 1,215,000 residents are without a job. Among these are university graduates and many young people.

A separate Quebec might well end up being thoroughly French, but its citizens would be immersed in a social, economic, and political crisis that would give the rest of the world an impression of frustration and despair.

Quebeckers, after the last referendum, were viewed as racists and fanatics. In fact, francophone Quebeckers are normally known for their openness and tolerance. The same cannot be said of our political élite, however, which remains disconnected from the public.

Remember, for instance, the less than favourable editorial comments published world-wide following the Parti Québécois' decision to prohibit the use of English on commercial signs. Bill 101 had the effect of turning the English language, which happens to be at the top of the list of languages most used around the world, into a minority dialect when francophones represent 1.8 percent of the population of North America and close to a million anglophones live in Quebec. How can we blame those who denounced the fascist nature of our legislation? The Supreme Court of Canada forced the Quebec government to amend Bill 101 and, as explained above, I took a stand against the separatist élite and supported the proposal put forward in 1993 by Claude Ryan. In the early 1980s, I also represented the municipality of Côte Saint-Luc in an action to amend those provisions of Bill 101 that prohibited elected members of a municipality from corresponding in English with their anglophone voters. I argued this case before the National Assembly's Parliamentary Commission which was chaired, at the time, by Gérald Godin; I won. These days, I am dismayed to see that the old language debate, which tore asunder the province for so many years, is resurfacing. What a terrible mistake! What a step back! It can only spell disaster.

The separatist élite's radical fringe seems to want to strengthen Bill 101's provisions and reopen this debate. The enactment is, of course, perfectly tailored to its stated purpose. Bill 101 does, indeed, protect the French language in Quebec.

Lucien Bouchard's government has (as of May 1996) decided not to amend the Charter of the French Language. I sincerely hope that this whole issue will not degenerate further and that the more moderate members of the Parti Québécois will manage to extinguish the frivolous bonfire lit by those who like to fan the linguistic flame in the hope that the francophone population will finally opt for independence. To bolster their creed, these radical party members often make use of divisive language.

Finally, the spontaneous nature of certain recent political speeches peppered with racist comments suggests that, above and beyond any official policy, racial intolerance has always been a part of the Parti Québécois' internal discourse. On the night of the referendum, on 30 October 1995, Jacques Parizeau, then Premier of Quebec, blamed the rejection of his separatist dream on "money and the ethnic vote." A few weeks earlier, Lucien Bouchard, then leader of the Bloc Québécois and our current Premier, mentioned those "women of the white race" who failed to provide Quebec with a sufficient number of children.

This latent form of racism is far from accidental. At the heart of the separatist project lies a rhetorical distinction between those of French blood and the others. Yet many immigrants have, in the past, allied themselves with the French. The Parti Québécois certainly holds out a hand to allophone, anglophone, and aboriginal citizens. It could not otherwise hope to preserve a positive image of itself.

Though it speaks of reconciliation, the Parti Québécois continues to harp on the fear that many francophone Quebeckers have of disappearing within the federation, of being assimilated or "colonized." Thus the party's attitude divides Quebec society, stands in the way of its progress, and portends the kind of climate that would prevail in an independent Quebec.

Given today's world, Quebec separation would be catastrophic. I discuss this further on. Several generations would pass before we could recover from the shock. Enterprises are already moving their head offices out of Quebec. Capital is being transferred elsewhere. Specialized workers are being lured outside our borders. Why would our brightest people remain where there is only bitterness, whining, and vengefulness when more attractive offers pour in from Europe or the United States? Clearly our specialized physicians, engineers, and fine electronic technicians will prefer to live and practise their vocations somewhere else.

Pre-referendum polls indicated that between 500,000 and one million people would leave an independent Quebec. A more recent opinion poll on behalf of the CBC/SRC and made public on March 25, 1996 corroborated these figures. More concretely, one out of every seven residents would abandon a separate Quebec!

Let's stop a moment to ask ourselves who these people may be. Are we talking about middle-class Quebeckers? Unemployed persons? Welfare recipients? The neediest among us? Of course not. Those who will go are the wealthiest and better educated of our citizens; those, in short, who will have the professional or economic means to move on. They will be sick at heart, but they will leave anyway, because they would rather not put up with the ensuing climate of frustration, despair, and intolerance, or with a society crushed under the weight of its economic, financial, social, and political problems.

Blueprint for a Modern, Prosperous, and Visionary Quebec

We already have everything we need to turn Quebec into a modern, prosperous, and visionary state. Now we need to believe that we can achieve this goal as a united rather than as a divided people. We must work to build a full-fledged state known for its moderation. How should we go about this?

WE MAY REACH SELF-DETERMINATION FROM WITHIN CANADA

Quebec's right to self-determination amounts to a right to determine its future within Canada. It does not, as some have claimed, amount to a right to secession. The right to secede, in international law, is granted only to colonies and associated territories. Neither case applies to Quebec. In every other instance, secession is a question of fact that the international community may or may not choose to ratify, depending on the circumstances.

We must know that we have a right to determine our life and future within Canada. We have, in fact, exercised this right many times since 1867. The French-Canadian people of Quebec founded Canada along with the inhabitants of Ontario, Nova Scotia, and New Brunswick. We should be proud of this country we managed to build; it represents our heritage. For the sake of our children, we must preserve our cultural, geographic, and economic patrimony.

Why, then, renounce our rights when we may, instead, contribute to the growth and progress of Canada? If we try to be objective about this — and I admit that, in the past, I may have been lacking in that respect — the answer strikes us instantly. There is no reason to demolish what we built. We must, on the contrary, be proud of the fact that we accomplished in a mere 129 years what no other country, except perhaps the United States, has achieved. Canada, its democracy, its values, its social and economic welfare, and its standard and quality of life are the envy of the world.

Quebec reached self-determination when it contributed to the founding of a new country called Canada without losing its identity, or allowing itself to be destroyed or cut down.

From within Canada, Quebec has made many decisions concerning its own future. In 1980, we said NO to René Lévesque's sovereignist plan. We decided against amendments to our constitution on the occasion of the Charlottetown referendum. Finally, in October 1995, we saw through a dishonest question and a systematic disinformation campaign on the part of the Quebec government, and chose to remain in Canada.

Clearly Quebec has the right to govern its own existence and has fully exercised this right on many occasions since Canada was founded. Quebeckers possess the right to live freely as citizens of a free country.

THE ROLE OF THE INTERNATIONAL COMMUNITY

In order to become a modern state, Quebec must also garner a certain degree of recognition from the international community. The question we must ask ourselves is whether Canada stands in the way of the growth, presence, or acceptance of Quebec on the international scene. Clearly Quebec does not need to secede in order to be recognized internationally.

Quebec already has the use of Canadian embassies abroad. It also makes itself known by way of its foreign delegations, the aims of which, besides helping Quebeckers on foreign soil, are to promote its interests and culture (and not its independence), and to present to future immigrants and foreign investors the benefits of a life on its territory.

Quebec also plays a fundamental role among French-speaking countries. Next to France, and because of Quebec's existence, Canada ranks second among the world's francophone nations. During francophone Summit meetings, to which Quebec and New Brunswick send their own delegations, francophone Quebeckers present to the world their own image of both Canada and Quebec.

We also have a role to play in other international organizations. Suffice it to mention the G7, the OECD, the United Nations, and the Commonwealth. Canada, of course, has a seat at the United Nations. When I was a separatist, we all dreamt of Quebec also holding a seat at the UN. Quebec, we told ourselves, would make her voice heard amid the nations' choir.

The truth of the matter is that because it is united to Canada, Quebec's voice in these groups is stronger than it would be if it were an independent state. Separation would narrow the circle of Quebec's influence in the international organizations to which Canada belongs. It would also do damage to Canada's position.

If we were to separate, we would certainly be excluded from the G7 (a group composed of the seven top industrialized countries in the world), whereas we now have the opportunity to affect the future direction of an organization responsible for major social and economic trends. The same holds true for the Commonwealth, in which Canada ranks second after Great Britain.

We also distinguish ourselves in our respective fields, as Céline Dion, Robert LePage, and Mario Lemieux continue to do. The Bombardier company, for instance, sells transport equipment around the globe and has just signed a contract to build a fast train linking eastern and western Florida. The drive shown by our heads of industry ensures us a place on the international scene. While Jacques Parizeau snubbed Team Canada's mission to China and India, Quebec entrepreneurs joined the team, established networks, and signed business agreements.

Will the separatist élite finally acknowledge our success and forge ahead without attempting to undermine everything we do? How much longer will we have to put up with its whining? Why always blame the federal government for our failures when our own successive régimes fail to live up to expectations?

A MAJORITY FRANCOPHONE CULTURE

Every modern state is known for a majority culture and civilization to which other cultures attach themselves. In Quebec, the francophone culture embraces and inspires those of the anglophone, allophone, and aboriginal communities.

The distinct character of Quebec is manifest in its full sovereignty over its Civil Code, its language, and its culture. Thus nobody may threaten our language or prohibit us from speaking, writing, or singing in French. We accordingly enacted Bill 101 to safeguard the use of the French language in Quebec and to limit access to English schools.

Our cultural industries are largely subsidized by pan-Canadian agencies. Studies indicate that if federal support of Quebec culture was calculated on a proportional basis in accordance with the number of Quebeckers living in Canada (25 percent), it would be reduced by 45 million dollars!

Our priority should not be separation, but rather the improvement of our language and school system. Not too long ago, Quebec films were translated into French before being distributed in France. That state of affairs could certainly not be blamed on Canada. If we insist on saying *"moé," "toé,"* and *"il fait fret"* instead of *"il fait froid"* to distinguish ourselves from the rest of the French-speaking world, then we should at least be honest enough not to blame *"les Anglais"* for the poor quality of our mother tongue.

We cut ourselves off from the francophone world community when we speak French poorly, and we cut ourselves off from the rest of the world when we fail to encourage our children to be fluent in the English language. We alone are to blame for the consequences of our neglect. We must cease pointing our fingers at everybody else; we have come to a point where we blame the Canadian constitution for our every misfortune.

It is not the constitution's fault that our college students do poorly compared to those of every other Canadian province. Only we are to blame for that. It is not the fault of the Canadian federation that the Montreal Catholic School Commission's high school drop-out rate is as high as 45 percent. And only we are to blame for holding the world record for teen suicide and the Canadian record for senior citizen suicides.

We have everything we need to be competitive, but if we fail to make use of all available means to succeed, then it is nobody else's fault. We must give up our habit of insisting that others carry the burden of our failures. Our belonging to Canada gives us the freedom to make sure that our culture, our language, and our francophone society flourish even as we respect other cultures and languages.

QUEBEC'S POLITICAL, LEGAL, ECONOMIC, AND FINANCIAL POWERS

Quebec, in order to thrive, must be endowed with the necessary political, legal, economic, and financial powers. Section 92 of the Canadian constitution grants us full jurisdiction over areas that are off limits to the federal government. Our political powers are, for instance, played out at the National Assembly. Our exclusive juridical powers give us free rein over the administration of justice and the practice of civil law on our territory. We are entitled to make decisions with respect to primary, secondary, and post-secondary education. Finally, our financial and economic powers have allowed us to establish distinct financial institutions such as the Caisse de dépôt, the Caisses populaires, the Société de développement industriel, the Société Générale de Financement, and the FTQ's Solidarity Fund.

The Canadian constitution endows us with all the powers we need to grow and to turn Quebec into a fully modern state.

A SHARED SOVEREIGNTY

Every modern state may share aspects of its sovereignty with other states. This is precisely what Quebec and Canada have been doing. Thus our central government manages the postal service, the military, foreign affairs, customs, navigation and shipping, and matters relating to citizenship and money.

Interestingly enough, the partnership agreement signed on 12 June 1995 by Jacques Parizeau, Lucien Bouchard, and Mario Dumont, and which Lucien Bouchard hopes to incorporate into the Parti Québécois' programme, practically amounts to a duplication of our present state of affairs.

This last point is developed further on. It remains that through this proposal a separate Quebec would share with

Canada her powers in matters relating to citizenship, customs, the free circulation of commerce, persons, services, capital, and the workforce, as well as Canadian currency, and all decisions pertaining to money. Quebec would also insist on acting jointly with Canada with respect to the following matters: transnational and international commerce, our representation abroad, internal transport, defence policies, financial institutions, fiscal and budgetary policies, the protection of the environment, decisions pertaining to arms and narcotics control, the postal service, and "any other matter that the parties deem to be of joint interest."

I ask my readers to consider the following question. Why separate and risk destabilizing Quebec just to recreate a partnership, the substance of which we may already rely upon, and which would rob us of the actual power we presently hold?

THE VARIOUS PEOPLES OF QUEBEC

Contrary to what separatists would have us believe, Quebec is composed of more than *one* people. The First Nations include a number of separate aboriginal groups, each of which forms a people. We must not forget the English-Canadian people, the French-Canadian people, and, quite simply, the Canadian people, who appeared on the scene in 1867 and has since included all peoples living on Canadian soil.

Greater confusion was caused by our introducing a new term in the early 1960s. We spoke, suddenly, of a "*Québécois* people." Since then, we no longer talk about French-Canadians; everybody knows that the *Québécois* are, in reality, the francophone people of Quebec. As much as we would like to believe that this new term includes anglophone, allophone, and aboriginal persons, it is only

39

because some will it to be so and repeat it *ad nauseam* that it is becoming true. The majority of anglophones, allophones, and aboriginals feel that they are full-fledged Quebeckers even if they hesitate to identify with the francophone cause, but they rally, above all, around the notion of a Canadian people.

By international legal standards, a people is a group of persons, the members of which enjoy a certain degree of self-determination, live within relatively well-defined boundaries, and are endowed with a common language, history, and religion, as well as with a collective will to endure and to resist assimilation. This definition applies to the francophone people of Quebec, as well as it does to the other peoples living in this province. The history and settlement of the English in Quebec dates back to 1760. Quebec anglophones settled mostly in the Eastern Townships, but many reside, as well, in the Gaspésie, the Outaouais region, and on the island of Montreal. This has been their territory for several centuries. Their will to exist is manifest in their resistance to assimilation. They have retained their own institutions, their culture, their language, their schools, and their hospitals. Similarly, the aboriginal peoples of Quebec are the guardians of their respective idioms, history, and territories. They, too, have resisted assimilation and have thereby shown their will to endure. They manage their own institutions, and their governments, though not fully independent, are to a certain extent free to determine the destiny of their communities.

The *Québécois* state includes all these peoples. The peoples of Quebec and of the rest of Canada are held together by the cement of the Canadian nation. They are united in their desire to improve their socio-economic condition, and by a common cause, which is that of Canada. Break up this cement, and Canada as we know it ceases to exist and we are all left fending for ourselves and our territories. Only a common objective, like that of Canada, can keep us united.

When I was a separatist who spoke of Quebec as a modern state, I used to insist that only independence could provide us with such a common objective. The world has changed, however, and we must not hesitate to revise our old convictions.

We must now choose between progress and regression. We can only go forward or back. We must decide whether we want to be close-minded and obsolete, or whether we wish to reach our full potential as an increasingly modern and dynamic state, and as a full-fledged member of Canada.

When I chose, on the eve of the twenty-first century, to give up on the outdated goal of independence, I truly knew that together we could rouse Quebec from its torpor and concentrate on modernizing our society. We must do it for our children, for we have a moral obligation to avoid transferring our frustration and our quarrels to the next generation.

CHAPTER TWO

Our Very Own Armchair Revolutionaries

(The Bourgeois Separatist Élite)

INSTEAD OF WORKING to build a prosperous and modern Quebec, the separatist élite keeps pushing a project that can only set us back. If we consider the pros and cons of separation, we quickly come to the conclusion that it is hardly worth its cost. We may even be unable to afford it. I outline in chapter 4 the arguments that convinced me that independence would amount to a social and economic catastrophe for Quebec.

I am quite certain that Quebeckers would not hesitate to finally turn their backs on this ruinous dream if they were made fully aware of its consequences.

Does Anybody Here Care About Independence?

The truth of the matter is that people are indifferent to Quebec independence; they are far more worried about the job situation.

A survey published in August 1995 in *Le Soleil* indicated that months after the pre-referendum campaign, and only two months prior to the referendum itself, less than 10 percent of Quebeckers polled said that they were interested in the subject of Quebec sovereignty. Fifty-two percent did, however, express some concern about the job market.

Our separatist élite, when it refuses to consider the dramatic consequences of the secessionist project for Quebec and Canada is, in effect, taking us down in a tailspin. How does this élite account for the fact that no more than 20 to 30 percent of the people of Quebec believe in the necessity of secession? Have separatists not been delivering sermons to that effect for the past thirty years? They even tried to reach their goal by softening the message with words like "sovereignty-association" or "partnership," though they carefully avoided explaining to the population the actual consequences of these choices.

You may wish to reply that 49.8 percent of Quebeckers answered the October 1995 referendum question with a resounding YES. We know now that the insidious and misleading nature of the question itself, along with the Parizeau government's systematic disinformation campaign, led voters to assume that a YES vote could lead to changes that stopped short of secession. A poll published on September 23, 1995 in *Le Devoir* indicated that one out of every three persons believed this to be true. According to the same survey, 28 percent of YES proponents thought that a sovereign Quebec would remain a province of Canada.

The Quebec population is not calling for independence. There is no bickering on city buses over this issue. There are no demonstrations in favour of secession. There is no separatist mass movement afoot. The élite, however, keeps using its power to get us to sing the same outdated refrain.

Can Independence
Bring Us Together?

What's worse, the independence option does not provide the people of Quebec with a hopeful, constructive project they could adopt. If, after the 1994 election, the Parti Québécois had really wanted to come up with a unifying scheme, it would have consulted Daniel Johnson's official opposition party, which obtained 44 percent of the electoral votes. The Parti Québécois could have asked the Quebec Liberal Party how far it was willing to go in order to come up with a formula that the population as a whole would be willing to endorse. Parti Québécois leaders could, in turn, have announced that they were relinquishing some of their claims.

It would then have been possible to present the Quebec people with a common project that they might have supported during the referendum. Such a project would have certainly proved successful.

We were, instead, once again unable to rise above our usual level of partisanship. We could not transcend the pettiness of our political scene, where Liberals are perennially pitted against *Péquistes*.

All this keeps eating away at our society and alienating friends and relatives. In many Quebec families, the secessionist cause has led to bitter disagreements: siblings, parents, and children have stopped speaking to one another. Someone told me about a husband who said to his wife, "If you vote NO at the referendum, it will be the end of our relationship; we'll have to get a divorce." Such grief over mere differences of political opinion. . . .

How can we tolerate a political scheme that divides our society and our relatives to that extent? This is unacceptable. We must reject independence if it brings us nothing but false hopes and carries within it the seeds of hatred and contempt.

Besides, who profits from our discord? Who instigated the 1995 referendum crisis though it was clear that no more than 35 percent of the population favoured separation? Who is at the origin of the squabbles that have torn apart Quebec families, neighbours, and friends? Who insists upon pushing the separatist cause even though Quebeckers' most ardent wish is to catch their breath before summoning the energy to rise to the challenges posed by education, unemployment, and the deficit?

A Bourgeois Élite Disconnected from the Needs of the People

We are being dragged in spite of ourselves into a dangerous and backward scheme because of a small bourgeois élite composed of career politicians, university professors, union leaders, reporters, and columnists who can afford to be wrong. Some are opportunists. Others actually make a living out of our constitutional conflict industry, or know that they will be the first to be offered a job on the morning after separation. Yet who will help the rest of the population find a job when our politicians are suddenly busy trying to keep Quebec from sinking? Who will help Quebeckers pay their bills, put food on the table, and heat their homes?

Like a fine piece of machinery, this separatist Mafia forms a network, the members of which are bound up with one another. The separatist machine was conceived to fulfill specific goals, among which is the ability to disinform, to create mass movements, to counteract statements, and to devise plans of action. Someone at the top of the hierarchy presses a button, and union leaders, reporters, university professors, politicians, and others with influence in their relevant fields swing into action.

Clearly this little élite manipulates events and information. The last thing on its agenda is a durable solution to the problems that undermine Quebec society. Everything is geared towards separation. Naturally there is no question of encouraging the people to move on to something else.

I cannot imagine Lucien Bouchard, Bernard Landry, or Gérald Larose suddenly pleading for a true reconciliation and saying something to the effect that "We realize that the people do not want to separate, and we have consequently decided to change. Instead of attempting to disunite our society, we will put separation aside, focus on uniting our citizens, and pursue, to the best of our abilities, Quebec's growth within Canada."

I asked those closest to me how they would feel if this scenario came to pass. Would they be disappointed, unhappy, depressed? Regardless of their personal convictions, most of the people I consulted expressed the hope that this day might come. They talked about it as if describing a lost dream. People want to be able to move on and focus on real daily problems without being perennially dragged, kicking and screaming, into a constitutional melodrama!

For the past twenty-five years, however, the separatist élite repeatedly tried to break up Canada as if it sought, in a determined and systematic manner, to make a crack in a dam.

Rather than waking up and acknowledging that the time has come to put an end to the gradual destruction of both Quebec and Canada, the separatist élite, deafened by its own rhetoric, continues to plot tactical campaigns to disinform, inebriate, divide, and intimidate citizens across the country.

At the opening of the Quebec Socio-Economic Summit, which took place between March 19 and 21, 1996, business-

persons told Lucien Bouchard that the political uncertainty
and threat of independence hanging over Quebec, instead
of being propitious to investors, was actually driving enterprises away and affecting the job market unfavourably.
Without skipping a beat, Lucien Bouchard retorted that
these entrepreneurs suffered from a "psychological block."
A few days earlier, Bouchard had declared that the separatist option had a life of its own and that nobody had a right
to shelve it.

It is, in fact, up to Quebeckers to choose or reject independence. Only they can agree to be led into a hopeless
adventure. The Bouchard government, in turn, has a solemn
responsibility to inform the population of the actual stakes
involved in secession. It must stop promoting an option, the
mere threat of which sets Quebec back several years.

Will the sight of a decaying Montreal and of a province
living in complete confusion and suffering unquestionably
from the threat of a third referendum finally incite our
armchair revolutionaries to reflect upon the situation?

La Presse's headline of March 29, 1996 read: "Quebec
retains poverty record." What a pathetic distinction! A
report made public on March 28 by the National Welfare
Council revealed that Quebec has the highest poverty rate
in Canada: 1.45 million Quebeckers, or 20.2 percent of
the population and 45.5 percent of those living alone, are
considered poor.

The message we may derive from these figures is clear.
Quebec's problems are not of a constitutional nature; they
are rooted in social and economic factors. The threat of
separation alone can make matters worse. Does the élite
grasp any of this? Of course not! How pleasant it must be
to prepare for independence knowing how little we risk.
How wonderful to be able to work out various scenarios,
draft a new constitution, or draw up residential plans for
our new Premier!

We are being dragged into independence by only a few hundred individuals in Quebec. These persons are found within the Parti and the Bloc Québécois, in some of our universities, in our unions, over at Radio-Canada, among the press, and, more specifically, among those reporters who sit in the National Assembly's media gallery and act like parrots when they repeat the inanities they hear daily in the hope of swaying Quebeckers to the side of independence.

These persons must be denounced, for they exacerbate the existing divisions instead of attempting to heal the wounds caused by the last referendum. They are certainly to blame for Quebec's present climate and for the moroseness felt among all segments of the population. Instead of working to improve things, they play with our fate to suit their purposes.

This élite should accept the fact that the people are not buying the separatists' cause and start focusing on other issues.

A Quasi-Religious Dogmatism

The separatist movement has become dogmatic. Ironically, today's form of self-centred, fanatical nationalism carries within it the seeds of dissension sowed more than forty years ago, when we grappled with religious issues. We knew then that in order to keep our families together we had to avoid discussing certain topics. We found it intolerable that a Catholic would join the Protestant or any other faith. These conversions were akin to treason.

Similarly, Parti Québécois members must "have the faith or die." Those who resist the party's creed are no longer deemed to belong to the family; they are cast out as traitors.

This is, of course, what happened to me when I went public to denounce the party's fraudulent strategies. My brother Rosaire, for instance, has since stopped talking to me. His reaction is typical of the garrison mentality common to other party members. Rosaire used to be one of Jacques Parizeau's closest advisers. He now fulfills the same role with Lucien Bouchard. His position, however, does not excuse his behaviour.

I left him a message on his answering machine on New Year's Day. I told him that his refusal to speak to me went against our mother's deathbed wish. My two brothers and I had promised our mother that we would meet at least once a year; we had vowed before her to remain close.

I proposed that we save our brotherly friendship. We could meet and listen, openly, to what each had to say.

Though I can no longer share it, I respect my brother's viewpoint. If he ever agreed to speak to me again, this is what I would say to him: "You work hard, which is good, and you fight for your beliefs." I would avoid trying to prove him wrong. He would, in turn, ask me a few questions, and I would tell him that a group of citizens and I founded Citizens for a Democratic Nation in order to set things right, and to sell Quebeckers on the appeal of Canada and on the advantages of being Canadian. He would listen to me too. None of this would be problematic, for we would refrain from judging each other. We could talk about our political journeys as if sharing the details of a difficult, but pleasant voyage.

We could also meet on condition that we avoid politics altogether. We could, for instance, discuss nothing but personal matters. "How are your kids doing?" we would ask each other. "How about your wife?"

Those unable to conduct themselves in this manner behave like religious fanatics who go out of their way to avoid their excommunicated friends for fear of being damned by association.

Some of my old friends like to pretend that I was not a member of the Parti Québécois for twenty-five years. They like to forget that I made waves, that I worked hard, that I wrote two books on the Quebec national question, that I drafted several reports, or that I personally represented René Lévesque in an action against *La Presse!*

A few weeks ago, I ran into a member of the judiciary who was once a friend of mine at the Parti Québécois. He refused to shake my hand and called me a traitor. I took his remark lightly and said that we were all democratically entitled to our opinions. He immediately replied, "Not only are you a traitor, but you deserve a traitor's fate." He was alluding to the death penalty. I was dumbfounded! How could someone I had considered a friend, someone who held the office of a judge, speak to me this way? We had led many battles together in the past, yet he now saw fit to threaten me in this fashion because I had changed my mind!

His conduct, like that of my brother or of some of my old friends in politics, is, at the end of the twentieth century, completely anachronistic. These incongruities are throwbacks to the religious dogmatism that dominated our society into the middle of this century. Still, when set against Canada's democratic tradition, the Parti Québécois' intolerance does not augur well for an independent Quebec.

The separatist élite has inherited the worst traits common to all religious fanatics. Its members are intolerant, unyielding, intellectually dishonest, and incapable of either growth or self-doubt.

Yet federalists are also to blame for our present climate, for they have so far had neither the courage nor the prescience to defend their ideas forcefully and honestly. In any other country, they would have hoisted the flag and sung their anthem proudly. Our federalists, however, have failed to defend Canada.

Why the hesitation to intervene? The Canadian reluctance to get involved in Quebec's affairs gives the impression that separatists are strong, and that they hold the reins. In fact, they are the masters of a house of cards that may well collapse at the slightest draught.

The Parti Québécois is already terrified of those various Quebec groups that wish to remain in Canada in the event of Quebec's unilateral secession. I know, from my days as a Parti Québécois member, that there are obvious breaches in the separatists' proposed solutions to problems raised by our borders with the rest of Canada. To our everlasting relief, federalists always remained silent on this point.

Recently, citizens who believe that it is crucial that Canada remain united have taken matters into their own hands. They refuse to become separatist pawns. The Parti Québécois is certainly irked by this sudden rise in popular activism. Party members were used to having the run of the place. For a long time, all they had to do was paint Canada as the enemy.

Have Quebec federalists learned anything from the narrow victory of the NO forces at the 1995 referendum? I sincerely hope so. The separatist house of cards will finally tumble down when all the Quebeckers who care about Canada stand up and fight, inch by inch, to disprove the daily lies told by the sovereignist élite. Only then will the truth come out.

Our Lords of Disinformation: From Patriation to Meech Lake, on Our Way to a Distinct Society

THE MEECH LAKE ACCORD AND THE RECOGNITION OF QUEBEC'S DISTINCT STATUS

The separatist élite has done everything in its power to keep Quebeckers from adopting a project other than independence. This élite has systematically fought against the constitutional recognition of Quebec as a distinct society, and opposed the adoption of the Meech Lake Accord.

Yet how many times have we heard that the Meech Lake failure and Quebec's unentrenched status is to be blamed on those big, bad English-Canadians?

While the Meech Lake Accord was being negotiated, separatists fought against it tooth and nail, for they knew that it signalled the end of their sovereignist dream. I was still a separatist then, and I know that we were largely responsible for the breakdown of negotiations at Meech Lake. Did we not, through our writings and speeches, try to instill fear into Quebeckers' hearts by spelling out for them the possible aftermath of the accord?

The Quebec political élite as a whole conveyed an ambivalent message to the rest of Canada, for the Parti Québécois refused to join forces with the Quebec Liberal Party over the issue of Quebec's distinct status. What the separatists maintained was that they were not a society, but a people, for only a people may have a claim to self-determination.

If our political élite as a whole had bothered to give the impression that Quebec had reached a unanimous decision on the matter, things would have turned out differently. Separatists were not, however, seeking unanimity. As a former separatist, I must certainly share the blame for this.

The Meech proposal provided us with an opportunity to adopt a common project. Yet because the proposal had been put forward by the Liberal Party, we decided once again to sow the seeds of dissension and to flaunt our confirmed inability to get along. We consequently fought this project and voted against it in 1989 at the National Assembly.

We were quite happy to see that Clyde Wells opposed the accord. When Elijah Harper voted against it at the Manitoba Legislature, thus single-handedly killing the prospect of unanimity among Premiers, we celebrated the event with champagne. We raised our glasses. "Bravo!" we told ourselves, "We won! We managed one more time to defeat Canada, and we still have a strong chance of obtaining independence!"

If the Meech Lake Accord had been ratified, the secessionist undertaking would undoubtedly have come to an end. Of course, people would have continued talking about it — we live in a democracy, after all — but the population as a whole, and our governments and political parties, would have been given an opportunity to concentrate on other issues. We could have gone on pursuing the development of our distinct society within Canada.

Ironically, the idea of a society possessing a distinct status within a larger entity was first put forward in 1981 by the Parti Québécois itself. Thus those who formulated the notion and took it all the way to the Supreme Court were also the ones who turned up their noses at the chance of seeing it entrenched in our constitution.

On December 9, 1981, the Lévesque government issued a decree that the National Assembly moved to adopt, and which was presented to the Canadian government. This document opposed the patriation of the constitution without Quebec's consent and featured the following words: "Considering that Quebec represents a distinct society within Canada . . . ."

The Supreme Court of Canada, in its decision of December 6, 1982, considered the matter of Quebec's right to veto the patriation. The Quebec government's attorneys, in the factum presented to the Court, made the following point:

In the context of the present reference, the word "duality" covers the overall circumstances according to which Quebec has, since the country came into being, formed a distinct society. It also covers all the guarantees offered in 1867 to the province of Quebec, described then as "the stronghold of the French-

53

Canadian people" and as "the sentinel of the French presence in North America." These circumstances and guarantees extend far beyond linguistic and cultural realms. Quebec society as a whole believed itself protected by the British North America Act. It knew, of course, that its language was protected, but it believed as well that this protection extended to its values, its laws, its religion, its education, its government, and the authority of its National Assembly over local matters . . .

In 1982, the Parti Québécois, which is known for its many contradictions, turned around and opposed the notion that Quebec may be a distinct society.

Prime Minister Jean Chrétien, whom separatists have accused of being a traitor, proposed that his government support the entrenchment of Quebec's special status, and suggested that each province do the same.

Once again, however, the separatist élite attempted to defeat the federal government's proposal by working against it and refusing to extinguish the fire it had lit.

Naturally, if it ever comes to pass, the Parti Québécois government will stand firmly in the way of a constitutional entrenchment of its distinct status. In Ottawa, the Bloc Québécois has already voted against the possibility.

The failure of the Meech Lake Accord, which would have granted Quebec a distinct status from the rest of the provinces, did more harm to the Quebec population than the 1982 patriation of the constitution, obtained without Quebec's consent.

How is it that federalists failed to explain to the population that the Meech Lake proposal, which could have brought Quebeckers together, and the patriation of the constitution, which raised more formal issues than it did substantive ones, were different and not comparable occurrences?

The separatist élite forces its ideological caprices upon Quebeckers and thus condemns them to a permanent state of insecurity. This élite keeps refusing to solve our problems and does everything in its power to make matters worse. It keeps us all from finding a lasting solution to the political instability prevailing in Quebec, which it insists on attributing to the rest of Canada.

THE CONSTITUTION ACT OF 1982

For years, Quebec clamoured for the "decolonization" of our constitution, which needed to be brought back from the United Kingdom and endowed with an amending procedure. At the last minute, however, successive Quebec governments refused to sign and thereby entrench the necessary accords. Such was the fate of the Fulton-Favreau accord and of the 1970 Victoria accord.

Yet it was imperative that this step be taken, for the Canadian federation would otherwise remain an unfinished work. Unfortunately, Pierre Trudeau had to contend with Quebec politicians, who either had no idea what they wanted, or who no longer wanted what they could have had.

Despite my reservations concerning the means used to obtain it, I must say that, in retrospect, the patriation of our constitution represented a step forward for Canada.

Though separatists blame the constitution for all their misfortunes, it does, after all, include the Canadian Charter of Rights and Freedoms, one of the greatest gifts ever bestowed upon Canadian citizens, since it entrenches their democratic rights and fundamental freedoms.

Thanks to the Charter, which acts as an invisible barrier between citizens and the state, every individual is henceforth sovereign. The Supreme Court, in turn, determines the distance that the state must keep in order to avoid infringing individual rights and freedoms. Any bill or statute that violates or curtails citizens' democratic rights or fundamental freedoms may be annulled, invalidated, rendered inoperative, or declared unconstitutional, unless the violation or curtailment is within "such reasonable limits prescribed by law as can be demonstrably justified in a free and democratic society" (Section 1 of the Canadian Charter of Rights and Freedoms).

The constitution is the supreme law of Canada. Any law that is inconsistent with its provisions is, to the extent of the inconsistency, of no force or effect, unless the Supreme Court of Canada, or a provincial or federal court, deems that the conditions found under Section 1 have been fulfilled.

The benefits of patriation were therefore considerable. I was, at the time, fiercely opposed to it, because I knew that the new amending procedure would preclude any unilateral declaration of independence on our part. Separation would hence be dependent upon the consent of Parliament and of the other provinces.

Still, separatists should have respected the Supreme Court judgement validating the patriation process. Instead, they led the people of Quebec to believe that they were not bound by our new constitution.

Ironically, in 1982, the Parti Québécois government opposed the federal decision to patriate the constitution without Quebec's consent and argued before the Supreme Court that Quebec had a conventional right of veto over the matter. Recently, the same separatist élite has been opposing Jean Chrétien's decision to entrench our veto power.

The *Péquiste* élite should, however, be pleased with Chrétien's efforts on behalf of Quebec, for it was, after all, René Lévesque (and not *"les Anglais"*) who forfeited our right of veto. Incidentally, Lucien Bouchard was, at the time, one of the Quebec government's attorneys.

In a legal memorandum dated December 2, 1981, I warned René Lévesque of the dangers of asking the Supreme Court to decide on the question of Quebec's right of veto. The problem, I submitted, was of a strictly political nature; it did not belong in the juridical sphere. The highest court in the land would, at the very most, sanction the legality of a constitutional patriation obtained without Quebec's consent. At the worst, it would hold that all provinces are legally and constitutionally equal, and that Quebec has no right of veto.

I was fully of aware of the importance of any court decision, so I argued that once the constitution had been patriated, federalists would also go to court over Quebec's decision to secede unilaterally in violation of the required amending formula.

René Lévesque decided to take a chance and go to court anyway. He lost and, predictably, the Supreme Court held that all provinces are legally and constitutionally equal, and that Quebec did not have a right of veto.

René Lévesque was a true supporter of the democratic process, and he knew that he would have to abide by the Court's decision. He knew, too, that his government had established a dangerous precedent by bringing a purely political question before the judiciary. From then on, the Supreme Court would have the authority to define and limit the extent of Quebec's powers.

René Lévesque also knew that, short of staging a coup d'état, separatists must abandon all hopes of a unilateral secession. The amending procedure written into our legally patriated constitution would see to that. Yet Lévesque was opposed to unilateral secession anyway. I discuss this further on in this chapter.

Separatists should have bowed to the Supreme Court decision. Instead, they characterized patriation as an act of force against the people of Quebec.

Let's be realistic: if Pierre Trudeau had waited for Quebec's blessing, we would still be without our own constitution. The separatist élite will never agree to any proposal emanating from the federal government.

Separatists are clearly unfair when they criticize Pierre Trudeau and Jean Chrétien, as they did on the eve of the 1995 referendum, for their roles in the patriation of the constitution. The patriation has been called an insult, an affront, and an offense to the *Québécois* people. To this day, separatists attack the manner in which it was attained without considering its benefits. There is nothing to be gained by this constant bickering over something that happened fifteen years ago.

AN INDOCTRINATED YOUTH

Regrettably, federalists allowed the Parti Québécois to re-write Quebec history. As a result, part of the population and some of our young people trust this distorted version of the past. During the last referendum, I saw with my own eyes our youth blindly following a political Messiah. These young persons never stopped to think or question the lies and falsehoods put forward by the Parti Québécois' propaganda machine.

Our young have fully embraced the cause of a separatist party that feeds them false hopes and allows them to think that secession will solve all their problems. I was once invited to speak at a conference in Boucherville. The audience that day was made up of 300 people, most of whom were adults. I asked those present why there were so few teenagers and young adults in the room. Where were our CEGEP and university students? Some parents answered that their sons and daughters would have liked to meet me, but that they were afraid to be the laughing-stock of their schools. They feared the reaction of their friends, who would have certainly jeered and said, "What? You joined the old federalist camp? That's so uncool!"

Separatists have indoctrinated our youth into believing that secession is "cool." It is so very cool to get rid of Canada, the biggest obstacle to Quebeckers' collective entreprise.

Sovereignty-Association Was a Euphemism for a New and Improved Federation

Some of you will tell me that what Quebeckers really want is a sort of sovereignty-association; something that would finally put an end to their constitutional woes.

René Lévesque was among those who wanted just that. Lévesque was not a true-blue separatist. He was far more partial to a complete overhauling of the Constitution Act of 1867. He wished to make sure that Quebec had entered a partnership with Canada before declaring independence. Thus the Parti Québécois had planned for two referenda in 1980, the first of which was meant to provide the government with a mandate to negotiate a form of association with the rest of Canada.

Quebec has, in fact, always been sovereign and a member of the Canadian federation. Sovereignty-association would have merely added to this existing scheme an upper house with a direct influence over federal policies.

This upper house would have included deputies or delegates from both the Quebec and Canadian governments. Together, they would have decided on the best way to administer common matters such as the military, the postal service, the seaway, a nuclear power commission, and other matters like our currency.

Thus we hoped that Quebec and Canada would, as sovereign countries, agree to co-manage certain defined areas, not as part of a constitutional arrangement, but on a contractual and renewable basis.

René Lévesque was mostly interested in shaking things up and bringing about reforms that were far less beneficial than some would have us believe. Those reforms would actually have set us back.

I can attest to the fact that Lévesque was sincere in his wish to negotiate a form of association with Canada before declaring sovereignty. Even before the 1982 patriation of the constitution, when the need for it seemed most acute, he was always opposed to a unilateral declaration of independence.

I was by his side when we founded the Parti Québécois; we had spent several evenings over at my place drafting various documents of a political nature. I had a great deal of respect for him, for he could temper the harshness of my separatist zeal. I thought that we should separate first before having any kind of a dialogue with Canada. I believed that the sovereignty-association project was doomed to fail, and that the rest of Canada would never agree to discuss even the first of our steps toward separation.

I nonetheless supported the 1980 referendum question and was asked to head the Athletes' Committee for the YES side.

René Lévesque found my views somewhat abrasive, but he knew that I eventually toed the party line. I realized that our differences had never marred our respect for each other when he asked me to "defend his reputation" in a 1983 defamation suit against *La Presse*. The case was settled out of court a few months before his death.

René Lévesque differed from Jacques Parizeau and Lucien Bouchard in that he held our democratic principles and the people of Quebec in the highest esteem. His wish was to guide Quebeckers through a gradual and consensual independence.

Conversely, in 1995, Jacques Parizeau and Lucien Bouchard showed a complete disrespect for the population and for our democratic principles and institutions. Parizeau and Bouchard knowingly lied to the public about the consequences of separation and attempted to arrive at a unilateral secession, which, as we now know, would have hurled Quebec into a severe crisis.

Their partnership scheme was yet another swindle meant to guarantee a referendum victory that would have led to unilateral independence.

Those who continue to believe that a third referendum might turn the clock back to 1980 must understand that sovereignty-association was merely a euphemism for a renewed federation, and that this can be achieved without resorting to separation.

Secession is unessential to Quebec's growth or to the evolution of Canadian federalism. It does, however, alienate a large part of the Canadian public, which looks upon it as an act of treason and as a rejection of Canada.

The truth of the matter is that the social and economic consequences of separation would be disastrous. Besides, secession would never gather enough popular support to become a truly unifying project. The price of improving our existing federation would therefore be high indeed!

Whose Interests Does the Bloc Québécois Really Further?

The Bloc Québécois is described in Quebec as an advocate of the people's interests. This statement, besides being patently untrue, is nothing but a smoke screen. The sole purpose of the Bloc Québécois is to infiltrate federal institutions in order to undermine Canada and help along the separatist cause. The Bloc is an accessory to a global strategy.

I can personally attest to this fact, for I was among the Bloc Québécois' founding members. It was established in 1971, shelved in 1972, and revived by Lucien Bouchard in 1992.

René Lévesque felt, from the very beginning, that planting a party like the Bloc Québécois in Ottawa would be nothing but a waste of time, energy, and money. History has surely proved him right.

Still, along with François-Albert Angers, Mathias Rioux, Louis O'Neil, Antonio Flamand, Henri Laberge, and several others, we founded the Bloc Québécois in November 1971. I entered its name into the official registry and was appointed president of its provisional executive. Yet given René Lévesque's lack of enthusiasm, and because we did not wish to split the party on the eve of a possible 1973 election, we decided to put our project on ice.

We had hoped that, once in Ottawa, the Bloc would strengthen Quebec's separatist movement. It was important to publicize independence on all possible fronts. Besides, only a federal party could have a say in matters generally of interest to Ottawa, such as our external affairs, our currency, credit, national defence, and the postal service. In order to get half the cake, we needed to be present in Ottawa on a daily basis, selling the benefits of independence. For this, we needed to elect delegates to the Canadian Parliament.

Our presence on the federal scene would ensure the survival of the separatist movement and allow us to promote the Parti Québécois as a party of the future set on political renewal. We knew, from watching the federal and provincial Liberal parties, that those with footholds in Quebec and Ottawa were more likely to succeed on the national stage. Conversely, the NDP would never come to power in Ottawa, for it had never established itself in Quebec. Yet though he followed the creation of the Bloc Québécois with a great deal of interest, René Lévesque decided that our plan was farfetched and would amount to nothing but a waste of time and energy.

The Bloc Québécois, revived in 1992 by Lucien Bouchard, had the same mandate as it did in 1971. Quebeckers were, however, successfully misled into believing that the federalist party was founded to defend their interests. In reality, the Bloc Québécois has but a single aim, which is to further the interests of the separatist élite.

Lucien Bouchard went on to exasperate the rest of Canada. I would even say that his party has clearly been prejudicial to Quebec's peaceable existence and growth within the federation.

The Bloc Québécois gives the impression that Quebeckers are indefatigable whiners. Worse yet, it seeks to destroy all hopes of Quebec maintaining successful relations with the federal government or with the rest of Canada. Bloc representatives, under Lucien Bouchard, voted against Quebec's distinct status and its right of veto. They criticize, without exception, every one of the federal government's moves.

The Bloc's presence on Parliament Hill also represents a sad chapter in Canadian history, for the party has nothing positive to offer Canada, and its members are totally uninterested in enhancing the nation's reputation. The Bloc Québécois' unavowed hope is, instead, to sap the Canadian Parliament from within until the entire federalist system collapses.

Bloc Québécois members criticize everything and everyone. They systematically reject every proposal that stops short of independence, even though it may be advantageous to Quebec or to the rest of Canada.

Bloc deputies ought to be ashamed of themselves for having voted against the recognition of Quebec's distinct status in 1996. Had separatists not spent the 1995 referendum campaign complaining that the rest of Canada had always denied Quebec that very same status? Had they not characterized this denial as "a slap in the face"?

All of this makes sense, of course, for separatists have always opposed the constitutional entrenchment of Quebec's special status. It is nonetheless regrettable that the Bloc Québécois, a federal party, would go out of its way to reject a constructive proposal put forward by the country's Prime Minister. The Bloc could have voted in favour of the motion while pointing out that further changes remained necessary. Instead, the party simply denied Quebeckers their special status. Besides being harmful, this type of behaviour is completely useless to Quebec's welfare.

The Bloc Québécois has, in short, failed to bring forth proposals that are advantageous to either Quebec or Canada as a whole. Does the Bloc's presence in Ottawa benefit Quebec workers? Does it propose to improve the lot of students, the unemployed, or our senior citizens? It does not. René Lévesque was right: the Bloc Québécois has amounted to nothing but a waste of time and money.

Separatists are in bad faith when they refuse to acknowledge that our system has its good features, or when they shirk their responsibilities and blame their errors and failures on others or on the constitution.

We need elected representatives with a Canadian or even a global perspective. We are not the centre of the universe, and we must stop dwelling on the wrongs we allegedly suffered. Our political representatives must evolve, set aside their parochial interests, and agree that, in today's world, problems must be tackled with a view to national and international solutions.

We Need to Turn Over a New Leaf

We must face the future. Why keep harking back to the same old stories about the Plains of Abraham, the Patriots' rebellion, the linguistic intolerance shown the French communities of Ontario, the 1942 conscription vote, the 1980 referendum defeat, and the patriation of the constitution? All that belongs in the past; let's now live in the present and ask ourselves what Quebec's real and present needs are. Let's ask ourselves where we have succeeded, where we have failed, and what we must do to change or improve our lives. The separatist élite is forever alleging that the federal government and the rest of Canada are opposed to Quebeckers' interests. It forever dwells on the past and thus neglects the present. Progressive societies, on the other hand, make peace with their past and move boldly into the future.

Quebec has, while remaining within the federation, obtained 90 percent of what the first separatists had originally hoped to obtain. Evidence of this can be found in the speeches delivered by Jacques Parizeau when he was still in power. He has always reminded us of our achievements. Well, bravo! Lucien Bouchard, however, keeps telling us that, despite our achievements, the Canadian federation is unsuited to our ends.

We may truly get everything we need while remaining a part of the federation. We need only apply ourselves to the endeavour and, above all, show a little good faith during negotiations. Threats, coercion, and blackmail are clearly unproductive. Canada is a young country, and though it has already achieved a great deal, it remains capable of further growth. We must believe that Quebec may indeed pursue its development in every possible field without separating from the rest of Canada.

Our separatist élite must put an end to its destructive strategies and to its incessant coercive statements to the effect that secession will inevitably follow on the heels of the federal government's failure to grant Quebec control over unemployment insurance or workforce training. It would be absurd to destroy an entire country over a wish for greater power. Quebec already holds all the tools necessary to protect its francophone identity and grow as a distinct society within Canada.

Federal politicians must, in turn, wake up and recognize that Canada will not always manage to withstand persistent attacks on its unity. As evidenced by the facts surrounding the 1995 referendum, the relentlessness of the separatist élite has already made a dent in the Canadian federation.

Quebeckers, instead of letting themselves be duped by Lucien Bouchard and other secessionist leaders, must also work together to turn Quebec into one of the most advanced states in the Canadian federation, North America, and perhaps even the world.

CHAPTER THREE

The Coup d'État

ON OCTOBER 30, 1995, we avoided by only a few votes a constitutional coup d'état planned by our separatist government. Had a majority of Quebeckers voted YES in the referendum, the Parizeau government, along with Bloc Québécois leader Lucien Bouchard, would have proceeded to split up the country unilaterally. This undemocratic act would have hurled Quebec into a serious crisis, the first innocent victims of which would have been Quebeckers themselves. Lucien Bouchard now tells us that he intends to initiate a third referendum. We must make sure that our leaders' conduct at the next referendum conforms strictly to the democratic rules essential to our political, social, and economic stability.

My aim in this chapter is to shed some light on the basic and important questions raised by independence. In doing so, I lay bare the undemocratic and fraudulent behaviour of the separatist élite throughout the last referendum. This behaviour led me to take the Quebec government to court in order to protect and publicize Quebeckers' rights. Indeed, without adequate information our citizens risk being led into a catastrophic adventure.

Can Separation Be Democratic?

There are only two ways of achieving secession in Quebec: one is democratic because it is constitutional; the other, given its unilateral nature, amounts to a constitutional coup d'état.

A FULLY DEMOCRATIC SEPARATION

Quebec's separation from the rest of Canada can be achieved democratically by way of an amending formula entrenched in our constitution. What this formula provides is that Quebec, if it were to separate, would require the consent of the Senate and House of Commons, and either the unanimous consent of all provinces or that of seven provinces forming at least 50 percent of the Canadian population.

Opinions differ on this issue. I myself believe that secession, to be democratic, requires the consent of the Senate and House of Commons, and the unanimous consent of all provinces. After all, Quebec independence would be the "amendment of all amendments." All powers held under the constitution by the federal government would have to be transferred to the Quebec government and to the National Assembly. It would also be necessary to abolish the office of Lieutenant-Governor and alter the composition and jurisdiction of the Supreme Court of Canada.

Had Lucien Bouchard and Jacques Parizeau wished to act in a democratic fashion, they would have planned an advisory referendum and drafted a question that could have been as simple and clear as "Do you wish to separate from the rest of Canada?" Had a majority of the population as high as 60 or 70 percent voted in favour of separation, our leaders would have been in a good position to put the constitutional amending formula to use and negotiate

Quebec's independence with the various governments of Canada. Naturally, a high level of popular support within Quebec would have influenced the outcome of negotiations. With a majority of Quebeckers championing the secessionist cause, the world community would have pressured the federal and provincial governments of Canada into giving in to popular demand.

Yet even if it proceeds democratically, Quebec will suffer serious economic setbacks following separation. I discuss these in chapter 4. A number of agreements with Canada, however, might soften the blow. A smooth, democratic transition from one legal system to another will also help lessen the risk of violent social conflict. The consequences of a democratic separation would be far less devastating than those of a unilateral secession.

THE COUP D'ÉTAT

In 1995, Lucien Bouchard and Jacques Parizeau chose to align themselves with the world's enemies of democracy. History will judge them accordingly. They attempted to secure Quebec's unilateral independence, which would have amounted to a forcible parliamentary and constitutional takeover.

On May 20, 1994, Lucien Bouchard told *La Presse* that "if Ottawa refuses to recognize us, we shall proclaim our own sovereignty and the rest of the world will sanction our actions."

Bouchard and Parizeau knew that they stood no chance of reaching independence democratically, for Quebec separatists can only rely on 20 to 30 percent of voter support.

Our separatist élite therefore decided to bypass Canadian constitutional requirements, violate the rule of law, and attempt a coup d'état regardless of the consequences for Quebeckers.

The Quebec government drafted a confusing question and conducted a massive disinformation campaign in the hope of winning the referendum by a 50 percent plus 1 majority. A unilateral declaration of independence by the National Assembly would undoubtedly have followed immediately.

To proceed this way would have been extremely dangerous.

We already know that the social and economic costs of independence are high, but what we may not know is that these costs would double if Quebec left the federation without the constitutionally sanctioned consent of its Canadian partners.

Barring the use of force, however, the new government of an illegally separate Quebec would be unable to impose its own constitutional order on those unwilling to accept it. How would such a government prevent various Quebec regions from pledging their continued allegiance to Canada? How could it avoid the parcelling up of its territory? What would it say to those who refuse to recognize the authority of its new juridical system?

Following the narrow victory of the NO forces in October 1995, many citizens became aware of the dangers of unilateral secession and decided to remain in Canada at all costs. How could anyone force these citizens to think or act differently if Quebec became independent through a unilateral secession?

THE RIGHT TO SELF-DETERMINATION

We keep hearing that the "*Québécois* people" has a right to self-determination. Often, this expression is equated with Quebec's alleged right to separate. I have already discussed this issue in Chapter 1, but I must elaborate upon it further.

Contrary to what the separatist élite would have us believe, a people's right to self-determination is not synonymous with a territory's right to secession. Again, only former colonies and associated territories may secede from a larger entity.

In other words, there is no general right to separate in public international law.

Resolution 1514 of the United Nations' General Assembly provides that "any attempt to destroy, partially or totally, the national unity and territorial integrity of a nation is incompatible with the objectives and principles of the Charter of the United Nations."

The matter of Quebec's right to secede was the object of a 1992 study conducted by five independent international law experts who considered the territorial integrity of Quebec in the event of separation. The study was ordered by the Secretary to the Commissions on the Determination of Quebec's Political and Constitutional Future, which were set up in accordance with Bill 150. These constitutional experts came to the conclusion that Quebec cannot invoke its right to self-determination in order to separate from Canada, for Quebec is not a colony, and it is deprived of neither its right to its own existence within Canada nor of her right to participate in the nation's democratic institutions. Thus "the notion that all peoples enjoy equal rights and have an absolute right to self-determination is one of the biggest juridical myths of the second half of the twentieth century. . . ."

For certain experts, the right to self-determination includes the right to form a state. Others believe, however, that the term has broader and less radical implications. To these latter experts, self-determination encompasses a people's "right to be recognized as such, to determine its own future, and to participate, within a larger state, in the democratic expression of the political will." In any event, the experts insist that the right to secession is inapplicable to noncolonial situations. Quebec, they add, is far from being a colonized territory. In fact, "the *Québécois* people exercises its right to self-determination within a Canadian framework; its claim to a prospective independence is juridically groundless."

It is important to understand that "there is no general right to secession in international law," for

> the generalization of the right to self-determination, defined as a people's right to found a state, would have dramatic, destabilizing, and obviously unwanted consequences for the international community as a whole . . . . In reality, the right to self-determination is and has been commonly known to mean that all peoples have a right to participate in the political, economic, social, and cultural decisions that affect them.

According to the experts, this last point applies most certainly to Quebec. In short, Quebec's will to separate is legally unfounded. So now what? Quebec may still "claim" its right to independence. The world community would then be presented with a *fait accompli*.

If this were to happen, however, "third-party states [would] reserve the right to deny the claim on grounds that the new state's existence is questionable or has been attained forcibly, especially if the use of force was backed in too obvious a manner by an outside party . . . ."

To conclude, secession is not a right generally recognized in international law. It is a question of fact that may or may not be ratified by the international community, depending on the circumstances. If the government of Quebec hopes to secede, it will have to do so in a democratic manner, by first obtaining the consent of its Canadian partners. A unilateral separation, because it would violate Canadian domestic law and the principles of democracy, would possibly unleash violent conflicts and incur the strong condemnation of both Canada and the rest of the world community. International recognition would not be forthcoming.

AN ABUSE OF DEMOCRACY

People often tell me that the independence of Quebec is a political issue that does not require legal sanction. Nothing could be further from the truth. The people of Quebec may ask for independence, but their demands will have to be processed along democratic channels. I therefore have no objection to an advisory referendum on the matter.

Of course, such a referendum would require that the people be asked a simple question: are they or are they not in favour of Quebec independence or separation? In the affirmative, the results would be used to negotiate an amendment to the Canadian constitution. Thus René Lévesque's 1980 referendum was perfectly legal.

In 1995, however, Jacques Parizeau and Lucien Bouchard had no right to ask Quebeckers to support unilateral secession without explaining to them what was at stake. Had they succeeded, they would have staged a constitutional coup d'état.

Parizeau and Bouchard asked Quebeckers to vote for sovereignty as provided for in a bill that would have given the Quebec government the authority to declare independence one year following the referendum in the event of unsuccessful negotiations with the rest of Canada.

Favourable referendum results would have authorized the National Assembly to act in flagrant violation of the Canadian constitution, and to take upon itself powers it did not possess. The Parti Québécois government hoped that a 50 percent plus 1 victory would legalize an otherwise unlawful step. Quebeckers would have then been the unwilling accomplices to this act of constitutional fraud. "The people of Quebec wanted this," our separatist leaders would have said later. "The people decided that we were entitled to usurp the entrenched powers of the federal government. The people finally let us know that it wanted us to proceed by way of a revolution."

I launched a lawsuit against the government of Quebec because the 1995 referendum was undemocratic. We should never assume that all referenda are democratic. It is always possible to take advantage of the people, and of democracy in general. Any referendum, the aim of which is to suspend individual rights and freedoms, can be characterized as an abuse of democracy.

The majority is not always right, either. What if the federal government decided suddenly to hold a referendum in order to strike down the powers of the Quebec National Assembly? What if a majority of Canadians voted in favour of the plan? Would Quebec leaders throw their arms up in the air and say, "oh well, if the majority wants it . . ."? Would media headlines read "Democracy rules in Canada"? I cannot overemphasize the fact that, in a true democracy, the people are not used by the ruling élite as unwilling accessories to unlawful acts.

How democratic would it be to initiate a referendum in order to ask the Quebec population to abolish freedom of the press for a duration of six months? And if the people voted YES, would the government be justified in enacting a statute suspending freedom of the press? Would this undemocratic gesture be made any more democratic by the fact that a majority had voted in its favour?

Imagine the Quebec government asking Quebeckers the following question: "Do you agree to do away with all taxes payable to Ottawa?" If Quebeckers answered YES, would that give the government the power to do anything about it? What if the question was: "Do you agree to prohibit the use of the English language in Quebec courts or in the

National Assembly, or on commercial signs?" Would it be democratic to go ahead with the prohibition on the grounds that 70 percent of Quebeckers had voted YES?

Clearly the matter of the independence of Quebec should not depend solely on a referendum.

Again, there is only one way of obtaining independence, and that is by way of an amendment to the constitution. Of course, it would be preferable to ask for the public's opinion first, but then a simple poll would suffice. The required amendment could be secured more easily if a high percentage of the population declared itself in favour of the project.

Naturally, the Parti Québécois government is aware of the fact that a vast majority of the people rejects the idea of independence, and so it keeps trying to come up with the right plan to persuade Quebeckers to agree to separation.

When I finally realized that the Quebec government was about to stage a coup d'état without letting Quebeckers in on it, I was shocked and disgusted. How could our government decide to ignore the constitution? How could it risk destabilizing Quebec? I was sickened, too, by the extent of the disinformation campaign launched to dupe the public.

The separatists tried to turn the people of Quebec into their unwilling and uninformed accomplices as they planned their constitutional coup d'état. Thus they swept under the rug the democratic tradition introduced into the Parti Québécois by René Lévesque.

FROM ONE REFERENDUM TO THE NEXT

Readers will remember that the matter of the constitutionality of a unilateral declaration of independence had been discussed already within the Parti Québécois. Prior to 1982, René Lévesque had opposed the principle, and had opted instead for sovereignty-association. After patriation, the constitutional amending requirements precluded any undemocratic and unilateral gesture on Quebec's part.

Jacques Parizeau's decision to initiate a definitive referendum leading to unilateral secession had been planned well in advance. Yet if Parizeau had told the Quebec public that he wanted to split up the country and that the risk of political and social chaos was high, only a tiny minority of Quebeckers would have agreed to his scheme. Besides being opposed to separation, the majority of the population wishes to preserve order and stability in Quebec. Quebeckers would have been justified in saying that the price to pay, and the risks involved in Premier Parizeau's plan, were far too high. The separatist élite was therefore faced with a major challenge. The people had to believe that the entire referendum process was strictly democratic.

Quebeckers hoped, on the day after the referendum, that they would be able to relax a little. Unfortunately, their hopes were short-lived. We now know that the Bouchard government intends to call a third referendum. Union leaders support his intention. CSN President Gérald Larose agreed in March 1996 that we must put an end to the political instability that prevails in Quebec . . . . Independence, he added, is obviously the answer. Quebeckers may have voted NO on two prior occasions, but our élite keeps acting as if those who refused to vote YES are responsible for the current political instability!

This time, the Parti Québécois will be even more clever than it was last year, and so we need to be far more vigilant. Lucien Bouchard appears to be more conciliatory and more democratic than Jacques Parizeau. He has expressed the hope that he may integrate the political and economic partnership project into the party's programme, he has met with anglophone and ethnic community leaders, and he seems willing to engage in fruitful talks with company executives and with the prime minister of Canada.

Some Quebeckers think that Lucien Bouchard will give up on secession. Others firmly believe that he will manage to negotiate an agreement with the rest of Canada before the next referendum.

We must understand that Lucien Bouchard's accommodating behaviour is purely strategic. Despite appearances, Bouchard is as undemocratic as Jacques Parizeau, for he participated actively in the decisions leading up to the last referendum. He is also being watched closely by other PQ members. The party's militant wing will call him to order if he strays from the party's goal, which is to achieve independence. Finally, the party is engaged in the preparation of a third referendum.

We cannot afford to be misled again!

Preparing for the 1995 Referendum

The Quebec government raced around the clock in order to attain independence. In just under a year, the government attempted to stage a coup d'état by way of a unilateral declaration of independence, to keep this plan from the population, and to use Quebeckers as accomplices in an undemocratic scheme that would have driven Quebec into chaos.

SIXTEEN STEPS TO A COUP D'ÉTAT

I have drafted below a short chronology of the events that led to the 1995 referendum. Readers may thus measure for themselves the depths to which the Parizeau government sank, as early as 1994, in order to deceive the public.

- *December 6, 1994: The draft bill respecting the sovereignty of Quebec is tabled at the National Assembly.*

77

Jacques Parizeau anticipated Quebec's unilateral accession to independence. He therefore announced that the draft sovereignty bill would be brought in for adoption before the National Assembly during the reopening of the legislature in September 1995.

• *January–March 1995: The Commissions on the Future of Quebec are set up by the Parti Québécois government.*

These commissions were set up to allow the people of Quebec to voice their opinions on the draft sovereignty bill. Most Quebec opposition and federalist leaders boycotted the commissions, which were soon denounced as massive propaganda operations. Those who dared speak up against independence were jeered, heckled, and subjected to sarcasm.

• *April 19, 1995: The National Commission on the Future of Quebec issues its report.*

Predictably, this report encouraged the government to proceed at all costs with unilateral independence.

• *March–May 1995: Opinion polls confirm that the majority of Quebeckers are opposed to separation.*

These results caused the government to revise its strategy.

• *June 12, 1995: Jacques Parizeau, Lucien Bouchard, and Mario Dumont sign a "partnership" agreement.*

This agreement represented the first step in the government's revised strategy. The Parti Québécois' purpose was to lead Quebeckers to believe that a YES victory at the next referendum would allow them to retain all benefits afforded by the Canadian federation (citizenship, Canadian currency, the free circulation of goods and services, capital, and persons, and so on).

- *July 1995: A formal notice is sent to the Attorney General of Quebec, Mr. Paul Bégin, and to Quebec Premier Jacques Parizeau.*

In this notice, I enjoined the parties to renounce their illegal referendum plans or to refer the whole matter to the Quebec Court of Appeal if they had any doubts as to the legality of their actions. I added that their failure to act upon my notice left me no choice but to take legal steps against the government of Quebec.

- *July 31, 1995: A formal notice is sent to the attorney general of Canada, Mr. Allan Rock, and to Prime Minister Jean Chrétien.*

In this notice, I asked the parties whether they had the intention of asking the Supreme Court of Canada to rule on the legality of the next referendum.

- *August 8, 1995: The attorney general of Quebec informs me, on behalf of the Quebec government, that he will not act upon my notice.*

- *August 1995: First pleadings before The Honourable Robert Lesage, J.S.C.*

I asked Mr. Justice Lesage to put an end to Quebec's referendum proceedings and to render a declaratory judgement to the effect that such a referendum posed a serious threat to the rights and freedoms of all Quebeckers.

- *August 31, 1995: Mr. Justice Lesage renders his first decision and agrees to hear the merits of the case.*

- *August 31, 1995: Quebec government attorneys withdraw on the instruction of the government.*

By this gesture, the Quebec government hoped to avoid having to deal with an unfavourable judgement.

- *September 5–8, 1995: Mr. Justice Lesage reflects upon the interlocutory motion I presented before him earlier.*

- *September 7, 1995: Bill 1 (An Act respecting the future of Quebec) is introduced before the National Assembly.*

Fearing an unfavourable judgement on Mr. Justice Lesage's part, the government of Quebec once again decided to revise its strategy and add to its original bill the partnership agreement of June 12. The new bill will not be discussed before the National Assembly, adopted before the referendum, or submitted for popular approval as planned.

Clearly the government hoped to confound Mr. Justice Lesage before His Lordship could render his decision.

- *September 7, 1995: The referendum date and question are announced at the National Assembly.*

- *September 8, 1995: Mr. Justice Lesage renders his judgement.*

Mr. Justice Lesage indicated clearly that the Quebec government's project was illegal and unconstitutional, for it aimed at separating Quebec from the rest of Canada by sidestepping the required constitutional amending procedure.

- *September–October 1995: The government of Quebec decides to ignore the judgement.*

Not only did the separatist élite ignore the judgement, but its members led Quebeckers to believe that separation by way of a referendum was perfectly democratic.

The federalist élite never made a public statement condemning this kind of conduct.

I devote the next few sections of this chapter to a more thorough scutiny of the issues raised above.

THE DRAFT BILL ON
QUEBEC SOVEREIGNTY

The draft sovereignty bill, which was tabled on December 6, 1994, was distributed to each Quebec household shortly before the winter holidays. Section 1 of the bill provided that "Quebec is a sovereign country."

Quebec's sovereignty was described in the explanatory notes as a necessary step towards a definitive solution to the constitutional quandary Quebec had been facing for several generations. The crowning irony of this draft bill was the following words: "It is proposed that Quebec become a sovereign country through the democratic process."

The Quebec government had also decided to hold a special referendum in order to submit the draft bill to popular approval after it had been adopted by the National Assembly.

There were to be six steps to the unilateral independence of Quebec:

1. Publication of the draft bill on the sovereignty of Quebec, tabled on December 6, 1994.
2. A period devoted to the informing and participation of Quebeckers.
3. Discussion of the draft bill respecting the sovereignty of Quebec, and passage by the National Assembly.
4. Approval of the act by the population in a referendum.
5. A period of discussions with Canada on the transitional measures to be set in place, with respect, notably, to the apportionment of debts and property. The constitution of Quebec would have been drafted at this stage.
6. The accession of Quebec to sovereignty.

Jacques Parizeau had announced that the draft sovereignty bill would be brought before the National Assembly at the reopening of the legislature in September 1995.

In fact, as discussed later in this chapter, steps 3 and 4 of the government's strategy were revised while Mr. Justice Lesage wrote his judgement in the summer of 1995.

In short, the government of Quebec had been planning for unilateral secession since 1994.

THE QUEBEC GOVERNMENT'S
BOGUS COMMISSIONS

On January 11, 1995, the Parti Québécois government set up its National Commission on the Future of Quebec, which was to organize hearings across the province so that individual citizens and interest groups could voice their concerns regarding the draft sovereignty bill.

It soon became obvious that these hearings or regional commissions were bogus. The Quebec Liberal Party and the majority of federalist leaders boycotted them. Those who testified at the commissions described them later as vast propaganda and marketing operations meant only to benefit the separatist cause. The government of Quebec never made a genuine effort to find the best way of amending the Canadian constitution in order to allay Quebeckers' fears. Certainly those who disagreed with the commissioners on the necessity of independence can attest to this.

As stated at the beginning of chapter 1, I myself testified before the Quebec City commission on February 15, 1995. It was on that occasion that I first came out publicly against the separatist project and asked the Quebec government to reconsider its plans. During and after my testimony, I was heckled and called names. The same happened to other citizens who sought to proclaim their allegiance to Canada.

A Boucherville businessman recounted for me his and his friends' appearance before his hometown's commission. This happened shortly before Christmas:

We were told that we had a half-hour to speak, but they cut us off after fifteen minutes when they realized that we had come to defend Canada.

As I told the commissioners that I was as proud as my friends to be Canadian, Jean Garon banged his head on the desk as if to say, "I can't believe this!" He held his head between his hands, shook it, and rolled his eyes. Everyone thought his facial expressions were hilarious. I kept on talking, because I was well prepared.

I was told after ten minutes that my time was up and that I now had to answer questions. I felt as if I was in a court of law.

The twelve commissioners started asking me rather technical questions — trick questions meant to annoy or confound me, or to make me look stupid. Yvan Loubier, the Bloc Québécois critic on matters related to the economy, had developed his own interrogation technique; his questions were quite sharp. Each time I was able to answer one of the commissioners' questions, they tried to prove me wrong or told me that I was being incoherent.

The question period lasted twenty minutes, and they did everything in their power to ruin my credibility, as if they were cross-examining me. I was able to unsettle them a few times, which seemed to offend them deeply.

I was made to feel as if I, a *Québécois*, was being accused of betraying my own country. You had to be pretty tough to put up with all that. I was alone before the twelve of them. Theirs was a pure exercise in propaganda.

Charles Desmartaux, the editor-in-chief of Boucherville's paper, *La Relève*, was next, and he was allowed to speak for forty-five minutes. He gave this lyrical speech on the need for Quebec to become sovereign. No one interrupted him; the commissioners were rapt with attention.

My presentation was then shown on the local community channel, but they took out the passages where I held my own against the commissioners. They only kept the ones where I looked hesitant. After they broadcast my appearance, Bernard Landry spoke for about thirty minutes and went on and on about democracy this, and democracy that. Such complete bad faith!

THE COMMISSIONERS' BIASED REPORTS

The National Commission on the Future of Quebec submitted its report to Premier Jacques Parizeau on April 19, 1995. Some of the commissioners' comments are worth pondering.

Consider the following, on page 14: "How, indeed, can we remain a part of a country that refuses to recognize the distinct character of its francophone founders?"

The commissioners must have suffered from amnesia when they wrote this, because the Parti Québécois has always opposed the entrenchment of Quebec's special status (see chapter 2). They also forgot to mention that Quebeckers have been able to grow within Canada and to form a society known for its francophone majority and endowed with its own laws, its own civil code, and its own financial and economic institutions.

Still, the commissioners never hesitated to reinterpret Quebec history. The following passages are telling:

Since Canada refuses to recognize the existence and the identity of the *Québécois* people, the latter has no choice but to resort to its own political affirmation. . . . [The existence of the distinct identity of the *Québécois* people] leads, logically, to the people's exercise of its right to self-determination, which is to say its right to determine its own future as a collectivity. (41)

The report also cast doubts on the impartiality of our tribunals and on that, in particular, of the Supreme Court of Canada. The commissioners wrote that "with the support of the Supreme Court, the federal government has continued to encroach upon Quebec's exclusive powers and to dismantle some of her laws" (44).

No evidence was offered to support these allegations. Perhaps the commissioners were referring to Bill 101, some provisions of which were declared null and void by the Supreme Court because they restricted the freedom of expression of anglophones.

Naturally, the patriation of the constitution was said to have led to "a complete breakdown in the trust that existed between Quebec and Canada for over a hundred years." Never mind the fact that the Supreme Court held that the Constitution Act of 1982 applies to Quebec. No one may question these separatist pronouncements.

Finally, in their conclusion, the commissioners recommended that the Quebec government proceed with its plan for unilateral secession.

A DECEPTIVE PARTNERSHIP

The polls in March 1995 indicated that four out of five Quebeckers wished to remain in Canada. As a result, the Quebec government decided to revise its strategy in order to better sell its separatist option.

On June 12, 1995, Bloc Québécois leader Lucien Bouchard, Parti Québécois leader and Quebec Premier Jacques Parizeau, and Action Démocratique leader Mario Dumont signed an agreement.

With only one exception, the contents of this agreement were similar to those of the draft sovereignty bill. The exception was the proposal of a political and economic "partnership" deal, the aim of which was to ensure that Quebec retain economic links with the rest of Canada and that a new political structure be created.

The partnership document signed by the three political leaders provided that the question posed to Quebeckers at the next referendum would mention that Quebec had the capacity to proclaim its independence unilaterally, and that the Quebec government would strike an economic and political partnership with Canada.

Clearly the intention of the document's signatories was to achieve independence at all costs. This partnership with the rest of Canada was deceptive; it was doomed to fail, for negotiations with the rest of Canada were to last no longer than a year. A Partnership Council composed of an equal number of Canadian and Quebec ministers would have allowed each side a right of veto, thus requiring unanimity in all decisions. Also, in the event of unsuccessful nego-tiations, the National Assembly would have taken it upon itself to proceed unilaterally with independence.

Naturally, this plan was unworkable. Jacques Parizeau and Lucien Bouchard were perfectly aware of the impos-sibility of concluding a transitional agreement with the rest of Canada in the year following a YES victory. They knew that the Canadian side would oppose the requirement that all Council decisions be unanimous. Given that Quebec represents only 25 percent of the Canadian population, Canada would also probably refuse to agree to an equal number of Quebec and Canadian negotiators. Just by way of comparison, the commission charged with negotiating the partition of Czechoslovakia was made up of a Slovak and two Czech representatives.

The purpose of this sham partnership was to lead Que-beckers to think that they could remain a part of Canada if they voted YES at the referendum. In reality, neither Lucien

Bouchard nor Jacques Parizeau had any intention of striking a deal with Canada before separation.

Consider, for instance, the statement made by Jacques Parizeau in the August 5, 1995 issue of *Le Soleil*: "Whatever the outcome of our discussions with Canada, Quebec will become sovereign once Quebeckers vote YES at the referendum. . . . English-Canada's response to the partnership offer is quite irrelevant."

Later, in an interview with *La Presse* published on October 19, 1995, Lucien Bouchard mentioned clearly that a YES victory would lead to Quebec sovereignty, regardless of the existence of a partnership with the rest of Canada.

Should any doubts remain on this issue, I remind my readers that Jacques Parizeau had prerecorded a victory speech in which he proclaimed, right in the first sentence, the "sovereignty" of Quebec.

Judges Are the Guardians of Our Constitution and the Champions of Our Rights and Freedoms

I realized, in the spring of 1995, what the Quebec government was plotting behind Quebeckers' backs. Federalists hesitated to react. I decided that I could not stand by and watch a coup d'état being staged. I made it my duty to use all the legal means available to fight this coup in the making. Having been a Parti Québécois militant myself, I knew that Jacques Parizeau was fully aware of the illegality of his proceedings. Still, these matters had never been debated in the media and I feared that the people of Quebec might be made to sanction an unconstitutional and catastrophic event without even realizing it.

Nothing and no one seemed willing to stop Lucien Bouchard and Jacques Parizeau.

In July 1995 I decided to appear before a judge and ask that my rights and freedoms, as well as those of millions of Quebeckers, be protected from the actions of the government of Quebec.

On July 31, 1995, I sent a formal notice to Jacques Parizeau and Quebec Minister of Justice Paul Bégin to apprise them of the illegality of their plans. What follows are excerpts from my letter to Jacques Parizeau:

Dear Mr. Parizeau,

Enclosed please find a copy of a letter I sent to the Attorney General of Quebec concerning the draft bill on the sovereignty of Quebec and any other referendum proceedings I believe to be unconstitutional and *ultra vires* the powers of the National Assembly.

I would appreciate your letting me know whether you have the intention of abandoning these proceedings or whether you hope instead to refer the matter to the Quebec Court of Appeal as authorized by law.

Should your answer be negative, I will have no choice but to proceed with all legal steps necessary to protect my rights and freedoms as guaranteed by the Canadian Charter of Rights and Freedoms.

Along with all other Canadians, Quebeckers are entitled to all the benefits and advantages bestowed upon them by our laws and constitution. . . . Though I am proceeding here on my own behalf, you will understand that my claims are made, as well, in the public interest . . . .

Comments by Jacques Parizeau concerning the government's intention to go forward with its plan regardless of Canadian reactions continued to crop up in the media.

In *Le Soleil* of August 5, 1995, Parizeau told Quebeckers that "the referendum deadline is near. We will be working on the next three months: August, September, and October, so buckle your seatbelts; we're taking off. We will get our own country."

Meanwhile, Quebec Minister of Justice Paul Bégin pretended to be unaware of the legal consequences of his government's behaviour, which seemed to embarrass him. He knew full well that Quebec's right to self-determination is not synonymous with an alleged right to secession. He knew, too, that I would not stand in the way of a consultative referendum. Still, in *Le Soleil* of August 8, Mr. Bégin's adviser stated that "Mr. Bertrand wishes to deny Quebeckers their right to vote. . . . Quebec's right to self-determination is indisputable."

THE RULE OF LAW

I thus appeared before Mr. Justice Lesage and explained to His Lordship the dangers and dramatic consequences of a constitutional coup d'état or revolution for both Quebeckers and Canada as a whole. Back in July 1995, I had hoped that the Court would issue a declaratory judgement to the effect that my democratic rights and fundamental freedoms, as well as those of millions of Quebeckers, were threatened by the government's referendum proceedings and by the prospect of a unilateral secession.

I cannot overemphasize the importance for any society of the rule of law, which can be defined as the respect of our constitution and of the other laws of the land. The rule of law is a cornerstone of democracy. Without it, we would be subjected to a chaotic, anarchic world in which only the fittest survive. We already know this, for, each and every day, we abide by the laws of our community: we pay our taxes, we follow traffic regulations, and we obey the dictates of our political institutions. Why should the politicians we elected behave any differently? Could it be that they stand above the laws of their country because they are part of the government? Does their position entitle them to breach our constitutional provisions? Certainly not! Even the government must obey the law.

This is what the Supreme Court of Canada said on the subject, in its 1992 *Canadian Council of Churches* decision:

> The rule of law is thus recognized as a cornerstone of our democratic form of government. It is the rule of law which guarantees the rights of citizens to protection against arbitrary and unconstitutional government action.

Unfortunately, Canadian Prime Minister Jean Chrétien, federal Minister of Justice Allan Rock, and Quebec opposition leader Daniel Johnson, who also led the NO forces during the 1995 referendum, seemed unfamiliar with the Supreme Court's statements concerning this fundamental principle. In the *Council of Churches* case, the court added that

> Parliament and the legislatures are thus required to act within the bounds of the constitution and in accordance with the Charter. Courts are the final arbiters as to when that duty has been breached.

Finally, in *Re Manitoba Language Rights* (1985), the Supreme Court specified that

> . . . the rule of law requires the creation and maintenance of an actual order of positive laws which preserves and embodies the more general principle of normative order. Law and order are indispensable

elements of civilized life. . . . The rule of law expresses a preference for law and order within a community rather than anarchy, warfare, and constant strife. In this sense, the rule of law is a philosophical view of society which in the Western tradition is linked with basic democratic notions.

Those who defy the rule of law may be the origin of chaos, anarchy, "warfare and constant strife." This may be Quebec's fate, if the Parti Québécois government decides that we are to secede unilaterally. We are not immune to increasingly bitter discourses that may lead to violence, and neither are we protected from the kind of conflict that has been ravaging Ireland. Yet unlike Ireland, where the armed struggle is conducted along religious lines, our civil war would pit separatists against those who fail to share their views.

Given our present circumstances, only a court of law can prevent Quebec society from being torn apart.

The Parti Québécois is known for its double standards. Section 8 of Bill 1 respecting the future of Quebec provides, for example, that a sovereign Quebec must be subject to the rule of law. What a total farce! How can the rule of law apply to a separate Quebec, but not to a Quebec that forms part of Canada? These inconsistencies are unacceptable.

QUEBEC IS BOUND BY THE CONSTITUTION ACT OF 1982

Some believe that Quebec is not legally bound by the 1982 Canadian constitution. I have already offered my opinion on the patriation of the constitution, but at the risk of repeating myself, I will say that René Lévesque, who was a true democrat, was opposed to a unilateral secession. Also, the patriation itself, along with the Supreme Court ruling establishing the equality of all provinces and the applicability of the amending formula to Quebec, precludes all arguments to the effect that we are not bound by our constitution.

Mr. Justice Lesage thus recognized that Quebec is included in the Constitution Act of 1982. To wit, he cites the 1982 Supreme Court ruling to the effect that Quebec is bound in the most unquestionable manner by the Canadian constitution and its amending requirements.

There is therefore only one way of attaining independence in a democratic way, and that is to fulfill the conditions imposed by our constitutional amending procedure.

The Honourable Robert Lesage's Decisions

(August 31 and September 8, 1995)

When I realized that the Quebec government hoped to stage a coup d'état, I asked Mr. Justice Lesage for an injunction that would put an end to the referendum proceedings, and for a declaratory judgement stating that the referendum would pose a serious threat to the rights and freedoms of all Quebeckers.

The only reason I asked the court to prohibit the referendum was that I knew that it would not be of an advisory nature, but would, instead, have decisive consequences.

THE ADMISSIBILITY OF THE MOTION

There was, at the outset, a hearing to determine whether the action was within the jurisdiction of the Superior Court of Quebec. Then, in his first decision of August 31, 1995, Mr. Justice Lesage agreed to hear the merits of the case, very much against the Quebec government's wishes.

The lawyers for the attorney general of Quebec (standing in for the government) argued that the courts should not meddle in the legislative powers of the government of Quebec and that they had no right of review over National Assembly privileges.

Mr. Justice Lesage pondered the question. We argued, in turn, that the National Assembly was indeed sovereign, but only with respect to those areas enumerated in the constitution. Unlike the parliament of a unitary state, the National Assembly had not been granted full sovereignty, and therefore had no right to make laws in relation to unlisted classes of people. Conversely, the Canadian parliament was not authorized to enact legislation affecting, say, the Sûreté du Québec, for the administration of justice and the capacity to regulate the Sûreté belonged to those classes of subjects assigned exclusively to provincial legislatures like the National Assembly. To each its own competence and sovereignty . . . .

Mr. Justice Lesage looked into the matter and dismissed the Attorney General's motion. His Lordship ordered that the parties proceed with the declaratory judgement and the injunction.

THE GOVERNMENT OF QUEBEC FIRES BACK

What did the Quebec government's attorneys, those fine jurists, do when they realized that they had lost the first round? They walked out of the courtroom! Never in my entire career had I witnessed such a thing.

They withdrew on the instruction of the Parizeau government so as to avoid having to recognize a decision that would have laid bare the latter's intention to stage a coup d'état.

The Quebec government preferred to act like a martyr and say, "we don't recognize the court's jurisdiction and we don't want to participate in the juridical debate on the question." The government sought to protect itself this way. Thus at a later date, it would have always been possible to add the following: "We couldn't recognize the court's decision because we were absent when it was rendered. What's more, the Superior Court is a federal tribunal presided over by a member of the judiciary who is appointed by Ottawa. This decision has no bearing whatsoever on our collective enterprise, which depends, instead, on the sanction of the international community."

During a press conference on September 1, 1995, Premier Jacques Parizeau even mocked the court:

> I must point out that Quebeckers' right to vote cannot be subjected to a court decision. This would be contrary to our democratic form of government. If we argued the case on the merits, as we are enjoined to do, we would most probably win, but we would also find ourselves in the absurd position of having to ask the court for permission to let Quebeckers vote.

"There will be a referendum," he added, "the people have a right to vote, and they will vote."

Jacques Parizeau always proclaimed loudly that he was quite certain his government would win the case in court. If that was true, why did he instruct his attorneys to withdraw? Why did he not press them to refute my claims? His refusal to engage in a juridical debate was a clear sign of cowardice.

While Mr. Justice Lesage pondered his decision, Jacques Parizeau changed strategies, thus telling His Lordship in an indirect way to mind his own business. Parizeau called an emergency meeting of the National Assembly. In a letter to the Speaker dated September 5, 1995, he emphasized that

The National Assembly will take all necessary steps to assert its rights, privileges, and prerogatives, to protect its undertakings from unwarranted interference, and to ensure that the people of Quebec will be given the opportunity to determine its own future.

On September 7, 1995, a new bill titled Bill 1 respecting the future of Quebec was introduced rather quickly at the National Assembly. This bill incorporated the partnership agreement of June 12 and conformed generally to the substance of the draft bill tabled on December 6, 1994. Yet the initial plan to submit the bill to a process of discussion and adoption by the National Assembly was omitted, along with the plan to have it subjected to a popular vote.

The Quebec government issued a decree on the same day to declare that the referendum would take place on October 30, 1995. The question to be asked was also made public and read as follows:

Do you agree that Quebec should become sovereign, after having made a formal offer to Canada for a new economic and political partnership within the scope of the Bill respecting the future of Quebec and of the agreement signed on June 12, 1995? Yes or no?

The Parizeau government thus hoped to unsettle Mr. Justice Lesage while His Lordship considered his decision.

Curiously enough, Bill 1 was mentioned in the referendum question, but it was neither debated nor approved by the National Assembly.

THE DECISION ON THE MERITS

The arguments on the merits of the case took place after Mr. Justice Lesage agreed to hear the action. In the meantime, and during the preceding weeks, I was subjected to enormous pressure. Threats — even death threats — were uttered against me. I was a hero to some, and, to others, a pariah.

Finally, my arguments drew to a close and, on September 8, 1995, Mr. Justice Lesage delivered a judgement considered among jurists to be exemplary. It amounted at the same time to an unequivocal condemnation of the Quebec government's actions.

To begin with, Mr. Justice Lesage, in his 43-page judgement, declared illegal and unconstitutional the process by which the Quebec government sought to secede from Canada without going through the required amending procedure.

Mr. Justice Lesage confirmed as well that the sovereignty bill, which provided for Quebec's unilateral accession to independence, posed a serious threat to the rights and freedoms guaranteed Quebeckers by the Canadian Charter of Rights and Freedoms. Most notably at risk were Quebeckers' freedom of thought, opinion, and expression, as determined and applied by the courts; their Canadian citizenship; their right to vote and to run for office in federal elections; their mobility rights, which include the right to enter, remain in, and leave Canada, the right to move to and take up residence in any province, and the right to earn a living anywhere in the country; their right to liberty and to personal security in the event of a disruption in the legal system; and their right to be treated equally and without discrimination by comparison with other Canadians.

Mr. Justice Lesage's statements deserve to be examined more carefully. His Lordship confirmed, first:

The legal system is a manifestation of the sovereignty of the state, which must ensure the allegiance of judges. The judicial branch exists in societies that recognize the paramountcy of the law, in order to have the rule of law respected and, most importantly, to have the acts adopted by the legislative branch respected.

His Lordship added that Quebec may opt out of the current constitutional system in one of two ways. The government may respect our constitutional amending requirements or stage a forcible parliamentary and constitutional take-over:

> These rules may be amended in accordance with the procedure provided for in the existing legal system, i.e. by acting within the bounds of the law, but they may be amended by means of an entity which places itself above the existing constitution and which has the physical control of the territory and the acceptance of the population which inhabits it.
>
> This last method is not legal. A new legal system can arise only after a fait accompli.

Having reaffirmed that the Constitution Act of 1982 applies to Quebec and that the Canadian Charter of Rights and Freedoms applies to the government "if the government's actions violate the rights and freedoms guaranteed by it," Mr. Justice Lesage noted that Quebec had no intention of abiding by the constitution's amending formula before separating from Canada:

> It is evident, if not expressly stated, that the government of Quebec does not intend to comply with the amending formula contained in the constitution in order to carry out the secession of Quebec. In this regard, the government of Quebec is giving itself a mandate which is not conferred upon it by the constitution of Canada.

The actions of the government of Quebec to achieve the secession of Quebec are a repudiation of the constitution of Canada.

If such an event were to occur, the Canadian Charter of Rights and Freedoms, which is part of the constitution of Canada, would cease to apply to Quebec, and the plaintiff would be unable to demand that it be respected.

His Lordship then established that the Quebec government's actions had an effect not only on Canada's political institutions, but on the constitutionally guaranteed rights of other Quebeckers as well.

In his conclusion, Mr. Justice Lesage held that the Quebec government's proceedings, which were meant to lead to secession, were manifestly illegal and unconstitutional:

The constitutional change proposed by the government of Quebec would entail a break in the legal system which is manifestly contrary to the constitution of Canada.

However, the clearly illegal actions of the government lead us to conclude that the plaintiff is entitled to a remedy which the court considers appropriate and just in the circumstances.

There is no doubt that the Quebec government hoped to stage a constitutional coup d'état, for it had decided to bypass the constitution's amending procedure.

Mr. Justice Lesage also established that the government may not seek the Superior Court's help to breach the constitution. Neither can the government utilize the National Assembly to enact laws, whose effect would be to tear apart the country. The National Assembly is a creature of the Canadian constitution; it was not meant to be an instrument of partition. Its role is to act upon those matters only over which it has jurisdiction. I submitted to Mr. Justice Lesage that the defendant had no right to use my National Assembly, paid for with my taxes, to destroy my country and abuse my constitution. If Quebec's separatist leaders wanted to step outside the bounds of the law and stage a coup d'état, they could always do it from a hotel room. Instead, they were using the National Assembly to give their actions the appearance of legality. Secession must not be confused with an ordinary legislative enactment!

I added that our official opposition had no right to participate in and be an accessory to this fraud upon the constitution. Its members had no right to sit in the legislature and say, in effect, "well, yes, the people want it. And so even though it is illegal, even though it is unconstitutional, we are going to participate in this great manoeuvre, in this coup d'état, because the people voted for it in a referendum."

Making citizens believe that it is quite all right to sit with great dignity before the cameras of the National Assembly and proclaim independence amounts to an unauthorized assumption of power. This kind of behaviour has nothing to do with responsible politics; it is a shell game, a Punch and Judy show!

Mr. Justice Lesage noted that none of the political representatives named as intervenors had filed an appearance. He also took judicial notice of the fact that all parties involved seemed to want to hold a referendum. Even I had declared that I would be in favour of a consultative referendum. Under the circumstances, His Lordship concluded that the issuance of an injunction to prevent the holding of a referendum "would risk creating greater harm than the harm that it sought to prevent."

In his declaratory judgement, however, Mr. Justice Lesage assumed that, even with a 50 percent plus 1 majority, the Quebec government would not declare independence. His Lordship assumed that, following a YES victory, our separatist government would obtain the agreement of other provinces and proceed to separate in a democratic fashion. In the end, Mr. Justice Lesage acted wisely, but he underestimated the deceit of which the separatist élite is capable.

The Uneasiness of the Political Élite

JACQUES PARIZEAU'S FEARS

Jacques Parizeau knew, on the morning after Mr. Justice Lesage's decision, that he found himself in a delicate position. The court's judgement amounted to a very stern condemnation of the Quebec government's actions. If the media and the federalist élite decided to exploit the judgement's conclusions, Jacques Parizeau would appear to be an enemy of democracy in the eyes of the international community and of the Canadian people as a whole.

With the help of Quebec Attorney General Paul Bégin, Parizeau decided to risk everything, and proceeded with a disinformation campaign meant to neutralize the effects of the judgement. Parizeau took advantage of the fact that Mr. Justice Lesage had refused to issue an injunction order. He argued that the court had allowed the government to proceed unilaterally with independence. Mr. Bégin even stated, in *Le Journal de Québec* of September 9, 1995, that "if the court had really believed that the referendum process was illegal, it would have issued the injunction order."

Mr. Bégin is an attorney. How could he have failed to grasp the true implications of Mr. Justice Lesage's decision? Worrisome as Mr. Bégin's attitude might be, it speaks volumes for the separatist élite's bad faith and for the current government's intentions. We must not forget that our current premier, Lucien Bouchard, participated in this extensive swindle.

As a matter of fact, both Jacques Parizeau and Lucien Bouchard insisted that the referendum was the embodiment of Quebeckers' democratic right to vote, and that the *Québécois* people could not be kept from determining their own future.

Yet separatists were saved once again by the apathy of our federalist leaders and of the francophone press. Unfortunately, the strategy devised by Jacques Parizeau and Lucien Bouchard was never denounced by Quebecois and Canadian federalists, who appeared, as usual, to be caught in the separatist web.

OF FEDERALISTS AND
MISSED OPPORTUNITIES

Federalist leaders remained quiet after the court decision, for they feared making a wrong move. Behind the scenes, however, congratulations poured in. I was told that the judgement was a pure wonder. The way in which I had conducted the proceedings in the face of tremendous pressures was characterized as a tour de force. Yet only a handful of people were courageous enough to say these things in public. Others were too frightened.

Regrettably, during the referendum campaign, the Lesage decision was never debated publicly by the leaders of the NO side. It is difficult to understand how these leaders, whose mandate it is to look after the rights and interests of the population, could take such a political risk.

There were, of course, obvious strategic reasons for this federalist silence. The opinion polls in September 1995 indicated that 60 percent of Quebeckers intended to vote

NO at the referendum. Why then risk confusing the public with these difficult questions?

It remains that we were on the verge of a coup d'état. We have, since then, narrowly avoided the possibility of a forcible political takeover by a few thousand votes, and all because our politicians were wary of informing the public of the issues at stake. This is an insult to the intelligence of Quebeckers, who are perfectly capable of understanding the importance of the rule of law and the significance of a court decision.

In what kind of a country would we be living today if, following a coup d'état, the Quebec government had adopted its own constitution? Would anyone respect this instrument? Many would probably say, "sorry, but we don't recognize your constitution any more than you did that of Canada. You may have included us in your Quebec, but we're out of here; we're going to avail ourselves of the right to self-determination and stay with Canada. You can do whatever you please; we're paying our taxes to Ottawa. We'll defend ourselves."

THE GHOST OF A
FEDERAL GOVERNMENT

Those who are interested in democracy will notice that the federal government did not participate in this debate. Even though the attorney general of Canada had been named as intervenor, our government in Ottawa failed to appear in court to defend the constitution. This is unheard of in such cases.

The government of Canada could have sent in an attorney to utter these simple words: "We believe in the rule of law and we therefore cannot allow things to go any further. We do not object to an advisory referendum, but we do object to the government of Quebec staging a coup d'état."

Instead, even after the attorney general of Quebec had asked its attorneys to withdraw, federal government representatives preferred to let a mere citizen stand alone before a judge to defend Quebeckers' interests.

At the time, however, the government of Canada believed that a significant majority of Quebeckers would vote NO at the referendum and that the matter would be settled politically. There is, of course, an obvious political dimension to the issue of Quebec's independence. Yet where is it written that we must ignore the legal and constitutional implications of independence? The law, as embodied in the constitution, is the very essence and substance of democracy.

The speech Jacques Parizeau recorded on the eve of the referendum is proof that Mr. Justice Lesage was overly optimistic when he assumed that independence would be achieved by way of an amendment to the constitution. His Lordship could not have foreseen that a Quebec premier would have the audacity to ignore a decision of the court.

In the same prerecorded address to the people of Quebec, Jacques Parizeau, who had anticipated a referendum victory, proclaimed the sovereignty of the state of Quebec. He spoke, as well, of reconciliation and of a partnership with Canada. He congratulated everybody. Yet at no point during his speech did he show that he had the slightest intention of complying with the court's ruling by seeking an amendment to the Canadian constitution.

Despite a crystal-clear judgement by Mr. Justice Lesage, Jacques Parizeau risked destabilizing Quebec. He decided to infringe upon our constitutional rules.

THE SILENCE OF THE MEDIA

The Lesage decision was translated abroad and was the topic of many international legal conferences. Quebec newspapers, however, failed to print the judgement in their editorial section. Normally, anyone who claims to speak on behalf of Quebec can get published in those pages. The media ignored the holding of a Superior Court magistrate, a representative of the judicial power entrenched in our constitution, who stated in no uncertain terms that we were neither legally nor democratically entitled to a unilateral secession. Why did the media never denounce the government of Canada's decision to shun the court proceedings or its refusal to comment publicly upon the judgement? Why did they never criticize the government of Quebec for ignoring the judgement? Why this silence on the media's part, and whom does it benefit?

A DUBIOUS MODEL OF DEMOCRACY

Apparently, American journalists were asked how the government of the United States would react to a judgement similar to that of Mr. Justice Lesage. The answer was immediate: the president of the United States would have respected the judgement because he believes in the rule of law and because the American public and the media would have otherwise called him on it.

In Canada, the political élite gets away with pretending that the rule of law is unessential to the stability of our society and to the survival of democracy.

World history is filled with examples of unlawful and unsuccessful attempts at unilateral secession from a federation.

Take, for instance, the case of Nova Scotia in 1867. Bolstered by a petition bearing 40,000 signatures (out of a total population of 50,000), the Nova Scotia legislature sought to separate unilaterally from the rest of Canada. This decision was brought before the Privy Council, which annulled the separation on grounds that it had been carried out without the consent of the nation's other three founding members, Quebec, Ontario, and New Brunswick. Thus Nova Scotia was made to return to the fold.

Towards the end of the nineteenth century, the British Columbia legislature enacted a statute, the effect of which was to allow the province to leave the federation. Canada disregarded the legislation.

Some time around 1860, the state of Texas attempted to separate unilaterally from the rest of the United States. Texas even went so far as to form a provisional government. An American citizen brought an action against the secessionist state before the United States Supreme Court, and the unilateral move was deemed illegal and null. The court held, in *Texas* v. *Wright* (1869), that Texas had joined the American Confederation with the consent of other states and that it would have to leave the same way. There were no two ways about it: Texas would attain independence with the consent of other confederate members, or it would achieve it by way of a revolution:

> The Act which consummated her admission into the Union was . . . the incorporation of a new member into the political body. And it was final.
>
> The Union between Texas and the other states was as complete, as perpetual, and as indissoluble as the union between the original states. There was no place for reconsideration, or revocation, except through revolution, or through consent of the states.

I was also told recently of a province of western Australia that had proclaimed its sovereignty following a provincial referendum held around 1938. The Australian constitution provided that a national referendum be held in such cases, so the Australian government took the matter to the citizens of Australia. The majority of Australians decided that western Australia had no right to separate unilaterally from the rest of the country. All parties abided by the constitution and the secession was annulled. Nobody complained that the entire process had been undemocratic.

In Canada, the composition of the federation can be altered only by an amendment to the constitution. Until further notice, this is the law of our land.

The Fraudulent Referendum of 1995

The government of Quebec lost its referendum: 50.6 percent of the population voted NO, and 49.4 percent voted YES. Yet our separatist government had spared no effort in getting a greater number of Quebeckers to vote YES. The government cheated when it asked an ambiguous referendum question. It had also hinted that an independent Quebec would remain a part of Canada. Finally, during the referendum campaign, the Parti Québécois government had managed to rally the support of Quebec's main unions, of its artists, of the Bloc Québécois, and of the Action Démocratique.

One month prior to the referendum itself, the results of a poll published in *Le Devoir* on September 23, 1993 indicated that 28 percent of those who intended to vote YES believed that a sovereign Quebec would remain a province of Canada. Only 43 percent of Quebeckers knew that the partnership agreement referred to in the referendum question was the political and economic partnership signed on June 12 by three of Quebec's political parties; 16 percent thought it referred to an agreement between the provincial and federal governments, 20 percent believed that the agreement concerned the wording of the question itself, and 21 percent had no idea what it was about.

Worse yet, it now seems that there were fraudulent, systematic, and Quebec-wide attempts at annulling as many NO votes as possible. Following an independent and detailed study on the number of rejected ballots (1.82 percent, or 86,501 votes), Messrs. Pinard, Orkin, and Kaczokowski revealed in an article published in *La Presse* of April 11, 1996, that "when looked at in the only possible acceptable manner . . . the allegations of electoral fraud, manipulation, and partisanship . . . are plausible . . . ."

Given the doubts raised by the actions listed above, which are, by the way, hardly coincidental, it is imperative that a public inquiry be launched in order that definitive conclusions be reached and that the culprits be identified. The following questions need urgent answers: Had orders been given across the province to reject unfavourable ballots and, if so, by whom? Exactly who was aware of this? The leader of the Parti Québécois? The government of Quebec? Its ministers? In the end, how is it that the government of Quebec never took it upon itself to launch such an inquiry?

Also, in a letter sent to the Canadian Armed Forces four days prior to the October referendum, Bloc Québécois deputy Jean-Marc Jacob suggested that Canadian soldiers join a Quebec army to be formed right after a YES victory! A House of Commons committee is currently investigating the matter.

Clearly these questionable tactics are indicative of the lengths to which the separatist élite will go to achieve its goals.

DEFINING THE WORD "MAJORITY"

Jacques Parizeau and Lucien Bouchard kept repeating that a 50 percent plus 1 majority of YES voters sufficed to declare independence. Quebeckers were confused about this, and the Quebec government did nothing to help them dispel their doubts.

Secession has seldom been attained in countries that have failed to obtain a 70 to 95 percent majority in their referenda.

Also, should the Quebec government ever decide to negotiate an amendment to the Canadian constitution, it will need to convince the rest of Canada of the validity of its project. A majority of only 50 percent plus 1 would be deemed insufficient. The separation project must be supported by a larger majority.

If the Quebec government could secure a majority of, say, 66 percent, Canada would have no choice but to agree to amend the constitution.

Thus the desired results may be obtained in a legitimate, legal, and constitutional manner.

THE NEXT REFERENDUM

Following the referendum of October 30, we believed that we would be allowed the luxury of focusing on other topics. After all, despite considerable confusion as to the true consequences of a YES victory, the NO forces had won.

We now know that Lucien Bouchard is planning another referendum.

On referendum night, after he had blamed the separatist defeat on money and the ethnic vote, Jacques Parizeau as much as told his supporters that he had no intention of waiting years before launching another referendum. "In a case like this one," he stated, "we have no choice but to roll up our sleeves and start anew. We won't wait another fifteen years!"

Lucien Bouchard echoed Parizeau's statement. "They haven't uprooted the sovereignist project," Bouchard told the separatist camp. "YES-side supporters had never been this numerous before. Let's keep our hopes up, for we will win next time, and next time may come sooner than some think."

Also, as mentioned earlier, Lucien Bouchard expressed his intention to go forward with the separatist project on the occasion of the socio-economic summit held in Quebec City on March 19, 1996.

This attitude on the part of our leaders is unacceptable. It can only be immoral to subject the Quebec population to anarchy, revolution, poverty, and unthinkable and unforeseeable difficulties. It can only be immoral to spend 100 or 150 million dollars on a referendum, which is what the government of Quebec did in 1995. Quebec has the highest poverty rate in Canada, and the Bouchard government is forever talking about the deficit, or about hospitals that must be closed down and social services that need to be cut. It can only be immoral to cause others harm, and the members of the separatist élite know, in their heart of hearts, that a unilateral secession would do permanent damage to both Quebec and Canada. The mere threat of secession is harmful enough. On March 21, 1996, on *Le Point*, a Radio-Canada television programme, Lucien Bouchard himself acknowledged that, despite his government's reassurances, the political uncertainty prevailing in Quebec was forcing investors to look elsewhere.

Back in Court Again

Quebec is not a banana republic. The judiciary must emphasize the principle according to which nothing and nobody is above the law in a democracy, not even a premier of Quebec or his government.

Nothing was settled during the last referendum, and we cannot afford to go back into the "bloody mess" from which we almost failed to emerge on October 30.

We must first assess our priorities and make sure that the Quebec government will never again be permitted to plan for the unilateral secession of Quebec.

Numerous citizens have asked me to defend their interests, and so I decided to pursue my action in court against the government. After all, the Lesage decision represented a temporary judgement that suspended all legal proceedings in the hope that the government might return to legality.

Thus in the amended proceedings filed on January 3, 1996, I made the following requests:

1. That all government actions leading to the referendum, including the draft bill respecting the sovereignty of Quebec, Bill 1 respecting the future of Quebec, all Orders-in-Council concerning the creation of the regional commissions under the responsibility of the National Commission on the Future of Quebec, all commission reports, the referendum question itself, and the results of the referendum, be declared inapplicable, unconstitutional, and null.
2. That the Popular Consultation and Referendum Act and the Electoral Act be declared inapplicable, unconstitutional, and null insofar as they may be used to allow or warrant unilateral action by the government of Quebec.

Also, in the amended proceedings to the motions for a declaratory judgement, a permanent injunction, and an interlocutory judgement, I request, on my behalf and on that of all Quebeckers who find themselves in a similar situation:

1. A declaratory judgement specifying that the government of Quebec's decision to proceed unilaterally with the separation of Quebec represents an illegal and unconstitutional action, that it amounts to a forcible constitutional takeover and a coup d'état, and that my democratic rights and fundamental freedoms are seriously threatened.

2. A permanent injunction to prevent the holding of all future referenda of a decisive nature.

The trial began on May 13, 1996, with a motion by the Quebec government's attorneys to dismiss the action. I cannot speculate here on what the judge will determine or on the unfolding of the proceedings. I will say, however, that I am surprised at the way the separatist élite keeps using terms such as "democracy," "respect of the law," and "rule of law" while flouting all of the above. The tactics used by this élite to bring Quebec to separation are undemocratic; they amount to a virtual coup d'état.

I decided to go to court to force our government to revise its tactics and show some respect for democracy, the rule of law, and the rights of all Quebeckers.

I call upon all sincere politicians to reflect, once and for all, on the implications of secession for our democracy. We must denounce any government that abuses our constitutional system in such an obvious manner. The people of Quebec must be protected against dangerous and illegal actions.

CHAPTER FOUR

Renouncing Independence

WE MUST ASK OURSELVES whether separation achieved through democratic means is desirable for Quebec. Separatist leaders claim that independence will allow us to overcome our alleged constitutional dilemma. The question is, do these leaders have the right to ask Quebeckers to foot the bill for their outdated dreams? They must realize that they have the duty to inform the public of the inevitable changes that will follow independence. Economic setbacks are unavoidable, and Quebec society will be further divided.

I invite my readers to look beyond the glittering dream of a separate Quebec — which, undoubtedly, many of my compatriots hold dear — and ask themselves what separation can bring to the people themselves. It is, furthermore, essential that we avoid the standard answers already provided by the Parti Québécois.

How about a "Velvet Divorce"?

Bernard Landry tried recently to convince us that Quebec was on its way to obtaining a "velvet divorce." The term has been used to describe the partition of the former Czecho-slovakia into the Czech Republic and Slovakia.

In March 1996, Lucien Bouchard expressed the hope that the 1995 political and economic partnership agreement be included in the Parti Québécois' program, but this move was clearly calculated to give the public the impression that the road to separation would be smooth and painless. We must remember that this partnership deal is a unilateral one, and that it emanates from a separatist élite that wishes to attain independence at all costs.

The government of Quebec thus hopes to give Que-beckers the impression that it is making sincere proposals to the rest of the country when it knows full well that Canada would reject these proposals. Quebec cannot conclude this type of agreement with Canada before separation, and separation would naturally unsettle both Quebec and the rest of Canada. Faced with Canada's predictable rejection of its "partnership" deal, the government of Quebec will doubtless state that negotiations with Canada are exercises in futility, and will proceed with separation.

It is true, of course, that the 1992 partition of the former Czechoslovakia took place with the consent of the two parties involved. The prepartition demands of Slovak separatists were staggeringly similar to those of our own sovereignist élite, and so there may be valuable lessons to be learned from this so-called "velvet divorce."

The polls at the time indicated that 30 percent of Slovaks favoured a kind of sovereignty-association along with the survival of a confederate link with the Czech Republic. Only 16 percent of Slovaks wanted a final, radical separation. The Slovaks had elected a party that used the threat of partition as a pressure tactic, but what Slovak separatists really wanted was to maintain their links with the rest of the country. They were caught at their own game when the Czech Republic called their bluff.

During negotiations, Slovakia proved a rather dismal failure at striking advantageous deals with the Czech Republic. Besides having always been stronger and more prosperous, the latter was better prepared for these kinds of discussions, from which it emerged the winner. A number of consequences followed. As a result of partition, Slovakia has suffered severe economic setbacks. Slovaks have witnessed a drastic decline in their standard of living, and they now regret their earlier decision to separate. They also miss being able to move freely across the entire territory without submitting to border checks. Finally, minorities are less adequately protected from discrimination. Ten months after the country's partition, opinion polls indicated that only 26 percent of Slovaks would have voted in favour of separation had a referendum been held on the issue.

Contrary to their wishes, Slovaks were kept from using a common currency. The Czech Republic had agreed to the principle, but the pressures from financial markets were such that the Slovaks were forced to mint their own currency, which is now considered weak.

The decision to open up common borders also fell by the wayside; numerous customs posts now keep a close check on the circulation of goods, services, and persons. This has led to sharp drops in commercial exchanges, industrial production, and the GDP (gross domestic product). In other words, Slovak life is far from what it used to be.

The apportioning of the national debt was drawn out and painful, and in the end the Slovak regime was unable to save as much as hoped for. Instead, public finances disintegrated, the deficit rose, and the cost of public services increased considerably.

Three years later, the Slovak economy is still reeling from the shock of separation, but the Czech Republic has resumed its growth.

We must draw the appropriate lessons from this example. Contrary to what Lucien Bouchard and Bernard Landry would have us believe, the Quebec population will, upon separation, suffer the repercussions of unavoidable economic setbacks. The aftermath of a unilateral secession such as that planned in 1995 by Jacques Parizeau would be even more disastrous for Quebec society.

Independence and the National Debt

In 1970, during the early stages of the separatist movement, the Canadian national debt was hardly problematic. By 1980, the year of the first referendum, it had risen to 100 billion dollars. Today, less than a year after the last referendum, the national debt (44 percent of which is owed to foreign investors) is nearly 600 billion dollars. Quebec can no longer afford to separate without witnessing a sharp decline in its economy and losing control over its public finances, which are presently in a state of disarray.

Quebec will have to absorb a considerable portion of the Canadian national debt, which it shares. It would be beyond the scope of this work to review all the studies on the issue, but it remains that, in the event of secession, Quebec would need to take on between 18 and 25 percent (probably 25 percent) of the national debt, which amounts to 150 billion dollars. This figure must be added to the 100 billion dollar debt engendered by the public and parapublic sectors.

Quebec will thus have to manage a 250 billion dollar debt at a period in its history when it will be contending with a serious economic crisis, and when its tax base will be lowered by the departure of a significant percentage of the population and an increased number of unemployed workers. The debt service, which rose to 11 billion dollars in 1992, would more than double!

Even more disturbing are the possible reactions of Canada's creditors, 44 percent of whom are foreign investors. Will they agree to exchange their Canadian bonds for Quebec bonds? This is highly improbable. Will Canada then remain these creditors' principal debtor? Will it assume the burden of payment, even though a part of it is really the responsibility of the government of Quebec? If so, Canada will need to impose a tax on Quebeckers until the debt is fully reimbursed, which is equally impractical.

Experts foresee that in the event of secession, the International Monetary Fund (IMF) will have to allay the fears of financial markets around the world by managing the apportionment of the Canadian debt and imposing a renegotiation of terms and fiscal policies. The conditions usually dictated by the IMF are quite stringent and difficult to meet. Besides, they would lead to the erosion of Quebec's monetary and fiscal sovereignty, which is what happened to Argentina. Quebec would thus be without the one kind of sovereignty that matters and might become even more dependent upon international financiers than Canada.

Allow me to get back to the question I formulated earlier in this chapter, and which I leave my readers to answer: Why risk destabilizing Quebec? Do Quebeckers have anything to gain from separation or is their goal in life to make the dreams of this power-hungry élite come true?

The Catastrophic Effects of Independence on Quebeckers' Lives

Responsible economists have no doubt whatsoever that independence would be disastrous for Quebeckers, whose standard of living would decline severely. In the passages that follow, I review for my readers certain of the important and unavoidable costs of separation.

INTEREST RATES WILL RISE

The increased Quebec debt and the creation of a new political entity will send risk premiums up and lead to a rise in interest rates. The people themselves will notice a sharp drop in their purchasing power and in their consumer capacity.

THE STARTUP COSTS OF INDEPENDENCE WILL BE HIGH

It would cost about a third of a billion dollars to found a new, independent state. Quebec would have to take on the added responsibility of all public services and areas currently managed by the federal government, including transportation and communications, taxation, defence, external affairs, the postal service, science and technology, agriculture, Indian affairs, public works, unemployment insurance, and so on . . . .

CORPORATIONS, LABOUR, AND INDIVIDUALS WILL MOVE OUT OF THE PROVINCE

We must remember that many corporations and specialized workers will certainly move elsewhere upon separation. The latter may be tempted to work in the United States, where salaries are higher and personal income taxes are lower. Many Quebec corporations have already left Quebec. This head office hemorrhage began in 1978. A period of relative calm and stability followed, but the exodus resumed on the eve of the 1995 referendum. Frequently we get news that a company has moved its head office to Toronto or to some other part of Canada while 50, 100, or 500 employees are left behind without jobs. We must add to the number of suddenly unemployed workers the accountants, attorneys, technicians, and consultants who used to gravitate around the departing company. There is no doubt about it: the closing of restaurants, hotels, and service bureaus will have a drastic effect on the economy of an entire region. Don't forget the countless individuals who will refuse to live in a separate Quebec. As previously stated, it is estimated that 500,000 to one million persons will leave the province as a result of independence.

THE UNEMPLOYMENT RATE WILL RISE . . .

Those economists most favourable to independence believe that the unemployment rate in a suddenly separate Quebec would increase by a minimum of 1 to 2 percent. What this means is that the deficit will grow by close to 2 billion dollars.

The rise in the unemployment rate will be caused by the departure of numerous corporations, and to a recession that will reduce the number of jobs available and cause several companies to close down.

. . . AND SO WILL SOCIAL EXPENDITURES

A higher unemployment rate and an increase in the number of welfare recipients will lead to a corresponding rise in social expenditures. Obviously, a greater number of unemployed workers means higher unemployment insurance expenditures. A larger number of welfare recipients means greater social welfare costs . . . .

TAX REVENUES WILL GO DOWN

The government of an independent Quebec will have to contend with an increase in social expenditures while being forced to agree to lower tax revenues.

Fewer taxpayers will be around. Some will have left the province. Others will have lost their jobs or will be unable to find one. Many companies will be doing business elsewhere or will be forced to close down.

THE ANNUAL GLOBAL DEFICIT WILL INCREASE

According to the most hopeful estimates, in 1995, an independent Quebec would have battled a deficit of 14 billion dollars, representing 8.3 percent of her GDP. Quebec would have then ranked just ahead of Italy, which ranks last among the world's industrialized countries.

THE ENSUING ECONOMIC
SLOWDOWN IS UNAVOIDABLE

The political uncertainty that would prevail in an independent Quebec, combined with increased interest rates, the flight of capital, the massive exodus of companies and individuals, as well as debt and deficit increases, would lead to a serious economic slowdown, to a decrease in tax revenues, and to increases in social expenditures.

Although some recklessly seek to minimize it, nobody can predict the extent and cumulative effect of this economic slowdown.

OPERATING EXPENDITURES WILL BE CUT

We cannot hope to address the disastrous economic effects of independence without mentioning cuts in operating expenditures, which economists estimate at over 3 billion dollars in the first year alone after sovereignty. These cuts will be necessary to ensure Quebec's financial accountability on the international scene. We are, after all, already reminded of the need to reduce the deficit from 5 to 2 billion dollars.

. . . AND LET'S NOT FORGET
THE FLIGHT OF CAPITAL

The flight of capital is harder to quantify, but it is already taking place in various sectors. Those who work in the securities market and attorneys working for large firms can attest to the fact that several hundreds of billions of dollars have left our territory both during and since the referendum. The threat of a third referendum can only exacerbate the problem.

What Will Happen to the Socio-Economic Welfare of the Citizens of a Separate Quebec?

How could we possibly do better than we are doing right now? Canada is among the seven most developed countries in the world. In 1994, Canada, as a member of the G7, ranked:

- *Third* for its gross domestic product (GDP), right after the United States and Germany.

- *Second* as a consumer society, after the United States.

- *First* for the overall quality of life on its territory (this according to a United Nations report).

- *First* for the socio-economic welfare of its population.

The people of Quebec know that Canada is unique; in an opinion poll published in 1995, 83 percent of Quebeckers stated that they believed Canada to be the best country in the world in which to live.

It will be impossible for a separate Quebec to rank so favourably among other industrialized countries. Is this not an additional reason to renounce a separatist project that can only lower Quebeckers' quality of life and their socio-economic welfare?

Will Independence Give Quebec Society Greater Control Over Its Distinct Status?

As stated in chapter 1, the Canadian nation is the cement that holds all of the peoples of Canada together. Many therefore want to know how Quebec's distinct status fits into this picture. After all, each province can claim a distinct history, a distinct geography, or a distinct population. It remains that Quebec is the only part of North America to possess a majority francophone language and culture, as well as a civil code that covers civil and commercial matters.

Quebec's distinct society can undoubtedly flourish within Canada. For instance, the people of Quebec are more than adequately protected. Their rights and freedoms are entrenched in two charters — the Canadian Charter of Rights and Freedoms, and the Quebec Charter of Human Rights and Freedoms. Quebeckers may apply to the courts every time that the rights and freedoms listed in one of these charters are violated by a statute. The courts may invalidate the infringing statute, and violations can also give rise to specific remedies. Quebeckers would hardly be better looked after in an independent Quebec!

Thanks to the French Language Charter, Quebec's distinct society also holds full sovereign powers over its linguistic and cultural policies. Bill 101 protects the use of the French language in Quebec. The Supreme Court of Canada established limits to the scope of the bill, for the freedom of expression and historic rights of Quebec's anglophones need to be safeguarded. Within these limits, however, the Quebec government can legislate in order to fully promote the use of the French language in the workplace, in schools, in hospitals, and in the courts.

There is no doubt that Quebec society is distinct, yet it is above all distinct within Canada. More specifically, we are known for:

- A civil code that is unique to Canada and which contains laws inapplicable to the rest of the country because they tally with our culture, our identity, and our specificity.

- Social programmes unequalled in the rest of Canada.

- Our respect for the historic rights of anglophones and aboriginals, as guaranteed by the Canadian Charter of Rights and Freedoms.

- The preservation and enhancement of the multicultural heritage of Quebeckers, as provided for under the Canadian and Quebec charters.

- Our capacity to choose, to a certain extent, the immigrants who will settle in Quebec.

All these characteristics make us different; ours is certainly a society that values and respects the important attributes of the anglophone, aboriginal, and allophone cultures that have taken root in our soil.

Would Our Sovereignty Be Any Greater in an Independent Quebec?

We live in a global world, and governments face increasing pressures as they try to solve societal problems. Contrary to what some may believe, absolute sovereignty, or the capacity to act exactly as we wish, is illusory.

These days, a nation's economy is linked intricately with those of a number of other countries. International investors may massively invest in or divest from a country within minutes. Companies may choose to settle in or leave Quebec, depending on what proves most profitable to them. Obviously, Quebec is susceptible to the fast-paced and shifting nature of our world, and Quebeckers, very much in spite of themselves, may suffer the consequences of a sudden state of economic chaos.

The duty of the government of Quebec is to secure the political and social stability of the territory and to give investors and companies the reassurances they need to remain and thrive within Quebec. It is also the responsibility of the government to ensure Quebec's future and harmonious growth.

I have often asked myself whether Quebec's sovereignty, after separation, would not be largely symbolic. What more could Quebec gain besides a flag, a national anthem, an official residence for the president of the republic, a fleet of embassies, and a seat at the United Nations?

Our sovereignty after independence would be emblematic, for Quebec is more sovereign and holds greater powers within Canada than it possibly could as an independent state.

Look at everything we already possess: Canadian citizenship; the Canadian currency; the free circulation of persons, goods, services, and capital; control over our economic future; the right to establish our own financial institutions; a strong voice with respect to the country's monetary decisions; a military presence; the right to participate in negotiations, signing and the arbitration of international accords; influence over international organizations, French-speaking nations, and the Commonwealth; and an exponentially greater capacity to solve cultural, economic, social, environmental, and geopolitical problems.

Why on earth would we exchange the undeniable power we hold from within Canada for a symbolic form of sovereignty that would leave us without real authority?

"*A Bird in the Hand . . .* "

Why have separatists always refused to accept the fact that we live in a unique country and that independence can only set us back dramatically?

When I was a member of the Parti Québécois, I knew that we were good at evading economic issues. We would tear into those who predicted financial catastrophes and accuse them of attempting to terrorize the elderly, the young, and the weakest members of our society. We told them that the economy was immaterial to our cause; what mattered was our desire to found a nation. It seemed essential that we extricate Quebec from what we perceived as a constitutional deadlock. We secretly hoped that economic problems would somehow get solved on their own.

Certain separatists declared themselves ready to make every possible sacrifice so that we might have a country and all the symbolic perks that come with it. They liked to add that Jacques Parizeau and Bernard Landry were economists, and that this would surely allay the fears of those who hesitated to vote in favour of independence.

We willfully ignored the economic evidence stacked against us and concentrated instead on our most sentimental reasons for wanting a separate country. We refused to conduct much-needed studies — serious and objective studies — on the economic future of this coveted country of ours because we knew that studies completed elsewhere only spelled disaster.

We must acknowledge that the separatist élite has always failed to act honestly and responsibly toward the people of Quebec. The studies Jacques Parizeau ordered from minister Richard le Hir on the occasion of the 1995 referendum were, in the eyes of the public, so clearly biased that they were shelved.

It becomes clear from the history of the last referendum that nothing has changed. The Parti Québécois remains fond of the old tactics, even if they often lead to disinformation. Jacques Parizeau and Lucien Bouchard made use of the same strategy we had used in the past: they appealed to the emotions of the public as they discussed independence, and accused those who spoke about the disastrous consequences of separation of wanting to "scare people off." In this respect, the publicity campaign generated by the YES side was rather telling. We were bombarded with posters bearing flowers, the "peace and love" emblem, a sign showing a construction worker, and the Canadian dollar. The message was clear: we would be just fine in an independent Quebec.

Unfortunately, Quebeckers are always taking the blame for these separatist games. Remember Jacques Parizeau's behaviour on the night of the referendum, when, in his capacity as Quebec's premier, he blamed the separatist defeat on money and the ethnic vote? In a speech prepared hours earlier in anticipation of a referendum victory, Parizeau actually congratulated Quebec's ethnic groups and private corporations on their impeccable sense of democracy. This speech was leaked to the press and published in our newspapers. Like Lucien Bouchard, Bernard Landry, and all the others, Mr. Parizeau kept trying to strike the sensitive chord.

We must put an end to this kind of behaviour. Sovereignty is a double-edged sword; the glittering, symbolic perks of independence co-exist with the real risk of an economic disaster. Our duty is to act responsibly and renounce the easy symbols of sovereignty in order to avoid obvious societal setbacks. "A bird in the hand is worth two in the bush" is the adage that comes to mind. We are clearly better off preserving our vested interests in the Canadian federation.

Some Quebeckers may be uncertain about the actual costs of separation, but we must nonetheless insist that our government give up its sovereignist project. We must also cease considering an option that risks driving us all into a crippling recession.

We already know that hundreds of thousands of Quebeckers would leave the province upon separation and that these unwilling exiles would be extremely difficult to replace. Some of them have lived among us for generations. Why should they, or anyone else, have to leave?

These Canadian citizens and full-fledged Quebeckers, the majority of whom were educated and trained in Quebec, will take their capital, their skills, and their families along with them. Years would go by before we could recover from the effects of this exodus. Can we afford to let a million or even half a million of our compatriots go into exile because of an outdated dream? We cannot! We certainly cannot afford to casually let go of a thousand, two thousand, or even ten thousand Quebeckers. That we could lose 100,000 or 500,000 of them is unimaginable. Given the price to pay, the separatist project is simply not worth it.

CHANGE VERSUS THE STATUS QUO

Many Quebeckers hope for change, but what does this really mean? During the 1995 referendum campaign, Quebeckers felt that they had to choose between an ambiguous "independence-partnership" package that reminded them somewhat of the old sovereignty-association of 1980, and the *status quo*.

We keep hearing that the *status quo* is the worst possible option for the people of Quebec. Let's be realistic and ask ourselves what it really entails. Is the *status quo* a disease with which we are all afflicted, and, if so, what are its symptoms? Does it keep us from eating, talking, writing, going on with our lives, or working for those who offer us work?

The separatist propaganda machine has appropriated the term for its own ends. We are led to believe that the *status quo* is synonymous with the alleged ultra-conservatism and rigidity of the federal system. Politicians, who fear everything, think of it as a virtual taboo. It is as if those who believe in Canada have caught this dreaded virus, which is eating them up.

In fact, the *status quo* means that Quebec will continue to thrive within Canada, which 83 percent of Quebeckers believe to be the best country in the world, and where the quality of life is exceptional. The *status quo* is in no way synonymous with stagnation. After all, our involvement in Canadian federalism has kept expanding since 1867.

Quebeckers claim to be unhappy because their successive governments have been unable to obtain greater administrative powers, like control over job training. They are unhappy because politicians are forever bickering over the same old issues instead of focusing on the basic problems facing our society. Well, Quebeckers are right, of course. We need to help our country improve. Yet this is a far cry from saying that we need to dismantle or let others dismantle an imperfect Canada.

Canada must evolve, but an amendment to the constitution is quite unnecessary. Quebeckers' needs and expectations can be met if we rethink the current division of powers and proceed to decentralize their administration. The federal government could also limit its spending power, which is viewed as an intrusion upon provincial competencies, work toward eliminating overlaps in the provincial and federal administration of certain areas, and enhance the efficacy of the Canadian economic union.

These improvements are necessary, and they may be achieved on condition that the Quebec and federal governments cooperate and act fairly. Given the flexible and adaptable nature of our federation, it would clearly be a mistake to choose separation over the *status quo*, which allows us to grow and flourish within Canada.

Even the most developed countries in the world have problems. We should look around us instead of always dwelling on our own predicament and coming to the erroneous conclusion that everything is hopeless. We need a sense of perspective: by comparison with the world's almost 200 countries, we have achieved so very much in only two centuries. Canada is our country; we need to work to preserve and improve its institutions.

CHAPTER FIVE

Learning to Live Together

QUEBECKERS ARE READY for the right kind of change. As we enter the twenty-first century, we want nothing more than to be able to leave our old quarrels behind so that we may live in peace and build a modern, just, and prosperous Quebec without the threat of separation hanging over our heads. We cannot spend our lives trying to separate. We must take the time to discover Canada, this nation of ours, and learn to live in harmony with Quebeckers of all origins and Canadians from every part of the country.

As citizens, our role is to snatch the old political debate from the claws of our political élite. The members of this élite too often abuse their power, misuse democracy for their own purposes, and manufacture artificial crises that seriously compromise our political, economic, and social stability.

This élite may have neither the capacity nor the desire to turn over a new leaf, yet its members need to abandon their obsolete dreams of independence. It is therefore up to us to help them embark upon a conciliatory course. Federalist leaders, in turn, must try to foster a healthier political climate. Their complacency, want of vigour, and lack of vision can only be detrimental to our society.

Quebeckers' fate should no longer be decided behind closed doors and drawn curtains. As they plan their future political agenda, our leaders must take into account the people's tenacious desire to remain in Canada.

We can only applaud Quebec Premier Lucien Bouchard for expressing his desire to make peace. We hope that he is sincere. Yet we would like to remind him that he too must close the chapter on independence and cease being an accomplice to his party's deceptive manoeuvres to get the public to agree to separation.

It will not be enough for Lucien Bouchard to secure a fragile consensus at various meetings and encounters where the dice are loaded with the threat of secession. The premier of Quebec must make sure that Quebeckers of all political stripes rally around a constructive project as full-fledged members of the Canadian nation. If he could accept the fact that Quebeckers have chosen repeatedly to remain in Canada, Lucien Bouchard would be in a position to solve many of our economic problems. Those dynamic forces in our society would then be able to unite in order to save Quebec from decay.

The Citizens' Power

We are on the eve of the twenty-first century, and it is up to us, the citizens, to speak up for what we want. We are indispensable players in a constantly changing world and the impartial arbiters of our society's needs. As such, we can work together and have a voice in the decision-making process. We are no longer patient and trusting observers, dragged by our leaders into a swamp from which they are now powerless to extricate us. We know that we are the masters of our own fate. We are aware of our leaders' shortcomings, and our message is clear: united, rather than divided, we can meet common challenges throughout Canada and the world.

I decided to do my part as a simple citizen and to take responsibility for the current political debate. I founded, along with others, a people's movement called Citizens for a Democratic Nation.

I became aware of the fact that the debate over political and social issues in our country never led anywhere, and that we therefore had to avoid placing our fate in the hands of politicians whose main concern is the result of the next election.

Politicians are dazzled by their own popularity and obsessed with polls. They forget that a society can progress only if its leaders focus on the future. They forget, too, that democratic rules must be respected, for they are the very bases of our society. Instead, our politicians abuse the power conferred upon them by the people and seem unconcerned with the fact that they infringe citizens' rights and freedoms. It is with a certain arrogance that they decide upon the fate of the population, as if playing a game of chess. In Quebec, political leaders act like vengeful and difficult children who keep asking for greater rights and powers without realizing that they also have obligations. They are forever dissatisfied, yet they fail to consider what they already possess.

If they were to gather and discuss these issues, citizens would be better able to put a halt to the downward spiral discussed in the previous chapters. Attitudes could change. Politicians could be pressed to govern in a responsible manner. Citizens could ensure as well that all governments aim for the greater political stability of Quebec, and that they respect our democratic principles and the rule of law.

A radical change of mentality is essential if we are to make progress.

The Voice of the People:
Citizens for a Democratic Nation

Our movement, Citizens for a Democratic Nation, was founded on January 9, 1996. In the next few pages, I set forth the text in which we define our common objectives. Our wish is to make sure that Quebec's growth and development are pursued from within Canada.

> Clearly politicians are reluctant to take steps to protect the Canadian nation and Quebec's existence within it. It is essential that we start listening to our citizens, who continue to believe that Canada is one of the best countries in the world, even if they acknowledge that modernization and improvements are needed to meet the challenges of the twenty-first century.
>
> Referendum proceedings undertaken by the Parti Québécois government were detrimental to the people of Quebec and Canada, whom they ended up dividing. The entire process was illegal, immoral, illegitimate, and undemocratic. A new referendum can only further weaken both Quebec and Canada. It is therefore important that we put a halt to this shameful waste of talent, energy, and money.
>
> Citizens for a Democratic Nation rallies Quebec and Canadian citizens who know that the existence and survival of a just, prosperous, united, and responsible society depends upon democracy being respected. Thus our members devote their time and energy to making sure that the democratic rights and fundamental freedoms of Quebeckers are protected, and that Quebec will continue to grow within Canada.
>
> In short, the movement brings together citizens who wish to ensure that, in the future, the democratic rules of our society are enforced.

OUR VISION

We believe that Quebec is a full-fledged member of Canada, which forms part of the heritage of all Quebeckers. We must work to thrive within this country we have built and which belongs to us all.

We are certain, however, that we cannot build a healthy, prosperous, and balanced society without acting in accordance with the constitution and the rule of law, both of which are cornerstones of democracy that keep citizens from the arbitrary exercise of power of the legislative and executive branches of government.

We further believe that the courts are the guardians of the democratic rights and fundamental freedoms of all citizens; that a referendum on the unilateral independence of Quebec has consultative value only; and that the referendum process set into motion by the Parti Québécois government in 1995 could have led to a unilateral declaration of independence, and thus constituted a fraud upon the constitution and a direct attack on the very foundations of our democracy.

We wish to make sure that, on the occasion of the next referendum concerning the future of Quebec, our leaders conform to democratic rules and consider the citizens' right to information. We feel that the separation of Quebec would set our society back many years. It is imperative that we learn to live together. Canadians of all provinces must accept each other as equal partners within the Canadian federation. They must cooperate as much as possible to improve and develop Canada while respecting mutual differences.

OUR OBJECTIVES

We must:

1) Sensitize Quebeckers to the importance of the rule of law in a democratic society.

2) Work toward the political, economic, and social stability of Quebec and Canada.

3) Ensure that any future popular consultation or referendum on the future of Quebec is conducted within the parameters of the rule of law.

4) Promote the advantages of being part of Canada over those of separation.

5) Inform Canadians from outside Quebec that the majority of Quebeckers reject separation as a viable option for the future.

6) Encourage Quebeckers of all origins and from all regions to get to know each other in order to learn to live together.

7) Highlight the immeasurable worth of the democratic rights and fundamental freedoms guaranteed by the Canadian constitution, and stress the fact that Canada is the most democratic country in the world.

8) Create links with other organizations that uphold the same principles both in and outside Quebec.

9) Recruit members from Quebec and the rest of Canada.

OUR ACTION PLAN

In order to protect and defend the rule of law and encourage Quebeckers and other Canadians to know each other better so that they may learn to live together, we dedicate ourselves to promoting the following activities:

1) *We need to reaffirm our common will to co-exist with the rest of Canada.*

We believe in and advocate the immeasurable importance, for Quebeckers, of remaining in Canada. Thus we feel that the time has come to reaffirm our desire, by way of a popular consultation, to live together as citizens of one nation.

Canadians from all parts of the country must be able to close the chapter on the past and voice their desire to live together in Canada and to honour their Canadian citizenship. This collective reaffirmation must take the form of a general federal election or referendum.

2) *We must convince the courts that, in the absence of a strong majority, a unilateral secession on the part of any province would be unconstitutional.*

We believe that our adherence to Canada is voluntary and that it is urgent that we clarify certain rules in order to prevent a seceding province from upsetting the democratic balance and stability of our society. We believe that a referendum of a consultative nature is acceptable, but that a referendum leading to unilateral secession is unconstitutional, for it imperils our democracy.

Mr. Justice Lesage held on September 8, 1995 that a unilateral secession such as that planned by the Parti Québécois is unconstitutional and illegal, and that it infringes upon the rights and freedoms of our citizens. Thus we find that priority must be given to the case of *Guy Bertrand* v. *The Attorney General of Quebec.*

3) *We need to promote a constitutional amendment that establishes the rules to be followed should a province wish to secede.*

The first step to such an amendment is a federal statute, the effect of which would be to

3.1) recognize the right of each Canadian province to secede;

3.2) establish the procedural conditions to the exercise of this right, namely:

a) that the seceding province obtain a significant majority on the occasion of a consultative provincial referendum (a simple majority of 50 percent plus 1 is unacceptable);

b) that a second majority be obtained in existing constituencies or predetermined areas of the seceding province, failing which said province must agree that the dissenting areas may remain in Canada;

c) that a precise question be posed that could read as follows: "Do you want X province to withdraw or secede from Canada? Yes or no?"

3.3) provide for pre-established proceedings to be followed in case of a vote favourable to secession, namely,

a) the formation of a team of negotiators composed of representatives from the seceding province and other parts of the country;

b) the establishment of a negotiation agenda and deadline;

c) the holding of a second referendum to submit negotiation results to popular approval;

3.4) establish non-negotiable conditions, such as,

a) the protection of minority rights;

b) the recognition of aboriginal treaty rights;

3.5) settle a number of critical questions, such as:

a) the issue of Canadian citizenship;
b) the currency to be used;
c) the apportionment of the debt;
d) all matters pertaining to transportation (by land, sea, and air).

The second step consists of ensuring that the above terms and conditions are entrenched in our constitution. The resulting constitutional provisions could read as follows:

1) This amendment to the constitution of Canada shall be made where so authorized by resolutions of the legislative assemblies of all provinces, and those of the Senate and House of Commons as provided under part 5 of the Constitution Act, 1982.

2) The Senate, the House of Commons, and all legislative assemblies that have agreed to this amendment may adopt such a resolution on their own despite a province's refusal to do so, but secession will come into effect only upon the adoption of the resolution by all parties.

3) An amendment to these new provisions concerning secession shall require the unanimous consent of all provinces, as well as that of the Senate and House of Commons.

4) *As we wait for the above rules to be clarified, we will refuse to participate in any proceedings that might lead to the unilateral secession of Quebec.*

We believe that it is essential that the democratic stability of our society be maintained. Thus as we wait for the above rules to be considered and clarified, we will refuse to participate in any action that might lead to the unilateral secession of Quebec.

5) *We shall sponsor a concrete plan of action to*

5.1) ensure the political, economic, and social stability of Quebec and of the rest of the country;

5.2) make sure that all parties act in conformity
with the rule of law, which is the basis of our
democracy.

A Useful Debate

MUST WE KEEP ON DEBATING THE
LEGAL IMPLICATIONS OF SECESSION?

Must we discuss the constitutionality of separation openly
and keep on denouncing the undemocratic nature of a
unilateral secession?

Some wonder whether it is necessary to set up specific
legal rules before another referendum takes place. They
believe, rather, in the importance of persuading Quebeckers to remain in Canada.

It is true that Canada forms part of the heritage of all
Quebeckers, who must be told about the enormous advantages of remaining in it. After all, together we can accomplish great things.

Yet we cannot hope to co-exist without having improved
our political climate. To begin with, those who advocate the
separation of Quebec must abide by pre-established rules.

Clear juridical precepts are essential to any democracy.
All parties must also live by these precepts. There can be
no country or democracy without the rule of law, which
remains the very basis for the existence of a healthy, responsible, and united society.

There are various reasons why so many refuse to discuss
the matter of the legality of a unilateral secession. Many

separatists fear that clearer rules will interfere with their plans. Some federalists think that Canadian unity may well depend on allowing a province to secede. Federalists have also been heard to say that it would be imprudent to publicize the implications of secession for our democracy, for it would only stir up old passions and lead Quebeckers to opt for separation.

I believe that it would be far more dangerous to avoid discussing the matter of the primacy of the law in the event of secession.

For instance, what would have happened during the last referendum if 50 percent plus 1 of the population had voted YES? Surely the results would have been challenged on grounds that the percentage of YES votes was insufficient to warrant separation, or that Quebec may not separate without the consent of other provinces. Aboriginal peoples and certain regions of Quebec would have demanded to remain in the federation.

The level of frustration among Quebeckers would have been high. Those who had voted YES would have been shocked to learn that they had not been told about the illegality of the referendum process or about the *Péquiste* coup d'état in the making. Those who had voted NO would have insisted upon remaining in Canada.

Clearly in this type of situation, the risks of conflict are tremendous.

The political élite must avoid being too cavalier about our democratic principles. It should never keep the entire picture from Quebeckers. Experience has taught us that a people deceived on a number of vital issues can only rebel once it learns the truth.

We will never be able to build a prosperous and united society if we fail to clarify these rules before the next referendum. We will continue to be subjected to the whims of our separatist leaders, who seldom hesitate to abuse their powers.

Why should it always be the Parti Québécois that makes decisions about the rules of the game, the wording of the referendum question, the percentage of votes needed to form a majority, or the date and the unfolding of the referendum? Separatists form a minority in Quebec. How is it that the majority of Quebeckers and the even greater majority formed by all other Canadians never have a say in the matter? Could these citizens not get together and declare that they reject the ambiguous wording of the question, or that they have their own ideas about the appropriate referendum date or strategy?

We must stop agreeing to these serial referenda ungoverned by predetermined rules. Why should separation not be subjected to certain conditions? Are there no terms and conditions to our belonging to or withdrawing from most associations? Are National Hockey League players from small towns and those from major cities like New York, Chicago, Philadelphia, or Los Angeles not bound by the same rules? Who would allow a particular team to start off with a couple of extra points? All teams play to win, under the best and worst of circumstances!

Political stability will return when these rules are made explicit to all. Only then will the government of Quebec be forced to conform to democratic principles. Only then will it be kept from planning for the unilateral secession of Quebec, from asking deceitful, ambiguous, and obscure questions, or from toying with what constitutes an acceptable majority.

These rules can be made clear by way of federal legislation, or through an amendment to the constitution. It will be necessary, at any rate, to specify that a referendum bearing on a province's decision to secede must feature a clear and unambiguous question. It is also crucial that a considerable majority of the population vote in favour of separation. This majority should be of at least 60 percent, which is more than reasonable when compared with other instances of secession in world history.

A regional majority of 51 percent would also be essential to ensure that the territorial borders of the new state are uncontested. Without this double majority, the risks of internal conflict and divisions are high.

The seceding province may fail to obtain the requisite double majority and nonetheless proceed to separate unilaterally. Should this be the case, those regions in which a majority was not attained will be able to remain in Canada. The ensuing partition of the territory will be thanks to those who decide to secede by infringing the constitution.

For instance, had the YES forces won the last referendum, Montreal, the Outaouais region, the Eastern Townships, the Beauce, and, possibly, some Cree, Huron, and other aboriginal territories would have continued to form part of Canada.

Partition would be catastrophic for Quebec, yet it would be inevitable given the fact that democratic rules had been violated.

What would happen if nine out of ten provinces agreed to the rules of secession, but the government of Quebec did not? Given the fact that Quebeckers have twice rejected separation, this kind of behaviour would be most undemocratic. Yet what recourse would the citizens of Quebec have at their disposal?

Citizens can boycott the next referendum and let the world know that the ensuing results carry no weight here or abroad, for they were obtained in flagrant violation of the rules determined by the majority.

Difficult as it may be to speculate on the future, it is certain that the duty and responsibility of the government is to solicit and agree to a clarification of the legal rules of secession before the next referendum. Meanwhile, our responsibility as citizens is to promote a fruitful dialogue on the issue.

SHOULD QUEBEC'S DISTINCT STATUS BE ENTRENCHED IN THE CANADIAN CONSTITUTION?

Prime Minister Jean Chrétien and his government ministers stated that they had done everything in their power to have Quebec's distinct status constitutionally entrenched.

Consensus is lacking on this issue. Many believe that the constitutionalization of a fact known and recognized by all would prove to be an exercise in futility. Others are still shaken by the failure of the Meech Lake Accord and refuse to discuss the issue altogether. Meanwhile, the separatist élite keeps rejecting the possibility of a constitutional entrenchment.

I mentioned in chapter 2 that the members of the Parti and Bloc Québécois have kept fighting the entrenchment of Quebec's special status, for they know full well that it would bring their secessionist plans to an end. I pointed out as well that they had succeeded in letting the population believe that *"les Anglais"* were hostile to the recognition of Quebec's distinct society.

There is no doubt that Quebec has managed to develop as a distinct society within Canada. All Canadians know this. Must we reopen this can of worms and stir up old passions again? Unless a majority of Quebeckers asks for it, there is no need to constitutionalize our "distinct status."

In fact, the Canadian parliament has enacted a statute according to which new federal legislation will from now on take into account the distinct nature of Quebec society. The federal government is bound by this law.

We know as well that Lucien Bouchard's government, along with the Parti and Bloc Québécois, have always opposed the recognition of this special status. In all likelihood, they will continue to oppose it.

Yet if the federal government decides to go ahead with its

plans to entrench Quebec's status, it will be necessary to define the notion clearly.

The term itself could be modified to do away with any ambiguity. "Distinct" does not mean "separate" or "independent." Thus Quebec could be described as "a majority francophone society or state" or as "a society or state made different by the language and culture of the majority, as well as by its civil code and institutions." The word "specificity" comes to mind. Recently, some have suggested that Quebec be referred to as the "main home of the French language and culture in North America," a rather cumbersome expression.

We believe that the term "distinct society" need not be changed. People have grown used to it; it is tolerated far better than it was ten years ago. Yet because the word "distinct," in English, can mean "separate," "distinct society" should perhaps be translated into English as "different society."

Whatever the words chosen in the end, people must understand that the notion of a "distinct society" means that Quebec society is "different from," and not "superior to," Canadian society as a whole.

Quebec does not need greater powers. It is capable of growing and administering itself fully by making use of the same powers held by other provinces. Legally and under the constitution, Quebec is equal to other provinces, just as other provinces are equal to Quebec.

I heard Bernard Landry and other Parti Québécois members say, rather contemptuously, that they were tired of Quebec being the larger equivalent of Prince Edward Island. P.E.I. may be smaller than Quebec, but it is the province's equal, and it benefits from the same advantages provided by the Canadian constitution. Similarly, Quebec, which is poorer than Ontario, Alberta, and British Columbia, is these wealthier provinces' constitutional equal. Are all Canadian citizens not equal regardless of their origins? A society's greatness is not measured by its territory's surface or by the number of people who live in it. What matters is the dignity, the heart, the intelligence, and the good faith of its inhabitants.

Legal and constitutional equality is not synonymous with homogeneity. Each province must develop differently, according to the cultural, economic, and social needs of its people. The Canadian family is akin to a human family in which each member grows according to his or her talents and personality. In the same way, all members of the Canadian federation are given the opportunity to develop and evolve in accordance with their capacities. Thus all provinces are distinct. Each province's territory, geography, history, or population is different from that of other provinces. Quebec has, however, been blessed with additional characteristics, such as its language, its culture, its civil code, and its institutions. Other provinces would not be doing Quebec a favour by recognizing its specificity; they would be doing Canada a favour, for our majority francophone culture effectively permeates all of Canadian society. It allows us, in short, to distinguish ourselves from the United States.

A Change of Heart

The twenty-first century is near. Isn't it about time that we put an end to our petty assaults on Canada, Canadians, and federalism? It is urgent that we become familiar with this country. Canada belongs to us too, and we should be proud of it.

We must also admit that the nation-state is an outdated concept. Quebec society no longer needs to separate from Canada in order to flourish. It can draw its strength from the talent, the generosity, and the passion of all citizens, regardless of their national origin. It can grow, as well, from the value given human dignity and from our recognition of the rights and freedoms of every individual.

Since the existence and survival of the French culture and identity are not at risk, Quebec francophones must understand that independence is needless. On the contrary, it represents a suicidal project that we must all battle energetically.

The separatist élite must face the fact that Quebeckers reject the kind of sovereignty that would take them outside Canada. They want to remain Canadian. They understand that they may reach self-determination in cultural, political, economic, and social areas.

Whether we live in Quebec or in the rest of Canada, we can only recover our lost confidence in the future if we accept ourselves as we are. Also, francophones, anglophones, allophones, and aboriginals must learn to be tolerant of each other's differences.

Canada is already the envy of the world. Imagine what would happen if we learned to accept ourselves for what we are, and if we worked together despite our differences.

As our mutual suspicions vanish and we are able to accept each other as equal partners in the Canadian federation, we will begin to push the limits of our potential and of our respective resources. Enthusiasm can only follow. Canadian citizens in Quebec and in the rest of Canada will come out winners from this change of heart.

Rediscovering Our Country

The history of Quebec written in the past twenty years has drawn our attention away from Canada. Let's face it: we helped found this country. We built it. We made it grow.

We gave it a name and a national anthem. Some will tell you that our history begins with the Conquest and that everything that follows from there must be aimed at redressing our defeat on the Plains of Abraham. This is a version of history to which I can no longer subscribe, for it provides us with a distorted sense of the past. Our history begins with Jacques Cartier, a French explorer who transcribed a Huron word — *kanata* — and gave our land a name: Canada. From then on, we were called *"Canadiens,"* then *"Canadiens français."*

The moment of our birth as a nation is a source of great pride; it cannot be erased from our collective memory. We are not a "conquered people"; we are Canada's founders. Later, our French ancestors travelled the continent. Champlain, Marquette, Joliet, La Salle, La Verendrye, and all the others were hardly fainthearted. They crossed an America that would come to belong to us too.

In time, French pioneers named the towns they founded across the country after themselves, their people, and their culture. Thus we have Maillardville in British Columbia, Gravelbourg in Saskatchewan, Île Madame in Nova Scotia, and Port-aux-Basques in Newfoundland. These days, we share this vast stretch of land with the aboriginal people who welcomed and helped us, with the English with whom, despite our differences, we have established the world's greatest democratic system, and with all those who joined us and shared with us the richness of their own culture. We are also linked genetically, for most of us can claim Indian, French, British, Irish, or other blood. This mix is our melting pot. We are bound by our common history.

Few other countries can boast of having such a rich background. Few are fortunate enough to belong to a land that stretches over a continent, and to be the citizens of a country envied and admired throughout the world. A month and a half following the referendum, in *Le Devoir* of

December 14–15, 1995, Edgar Pisani, a former minister under General de Gaulle, and a former senator and member of the European parliament, rendered a rousing homage to our country.

Pisani wrote that from the mouth of the St. Lawrence River to the Island of Vancouver, and from the Great North to the Great Lakes, Canada has founded a civilization, a state of being, and a way of life that are unique:

> What first strikes visitors, or even those familiar with the place, is the peaceable character of a people that knows nothing of violence or excess emotions. Here you will encounter nothing but respect and harmony — the respect that beings show one another, and the harmonious organization of a territory and its buildings. . . . You will delight in the sharp curiosity manifested by all citizens, and in their openness to all that is new under the sun. . . . You will be struck by the unaffected disposition of persons of all races and origins. You will be awed by the respect that Canadians show nature. You will be filled with admiration for the fierce, tireless, yet unrebellious, unsubmissive, and unpresumptuous struggle that women have made so that they may have a place in society, and so that their vision of the world and their ideas be taken seriously. And I did say their ideas, for in this country, freedom and equality are paramount. People in Canada are not, among other things, tolerant; they *are* tolerance and respect. It is a wonderful thing to watch and a wonderful thing to know!

This country belongs to us by virtue of our history, by right, and because it has captured our minds and our hearts. To lose it would be to lose a part of ourselves, to live through an intolerable tragedy. We would never recover from the sorrow of this loss. Canada is not an accident. Through Canada we have expressed our will to survive and to achieve great things as a nation. Canada represents our collective experience. You may tell those who say that Canada is nothing but a rotten deal that our present accomplishments are the sum of the contributions made by all citizens, including our modern-day pioneers. These citizens come from all provinces and distinguish themselves in a variety of disciplines, from industry to commerce, from education to medicine, and from telecommunications to sports and entertainment. Together we have learned what it means to share. We have learned the meaning of peace and progress. We have worked together to attain the exceptional quality of life we enjoy. We want to be able to pursue our achievements so that we may leave our children a country that leads the way in matters of tolerance, progress, equality, and justice.

It is thanks to the Canadian sense of justice and good will that Quebeckers spearhead this country. It is also thanks to Canadian democracy, which we have established together, that the official opposition of the House of Commons is made up entirely of Quebeckers known for the relentlessness of their efforts to weaken our country. These days, our anglophone compatriots and young immigrants from across Canada choose to attend French-immersion classes. The French language has never been so popular on this continent; never have there been so many people speaking it. A language that gains ground is not a language struggling for survival; it is a living, thriving language. The French language is part and parcel of the Canadian identity, and this is why, besides living in Canada, Quebeckers and all other Franco-Canadians *are* Canada.

GUY BERTRAND v. THE HONORABLE PAUL BÉGIN et al.

Superior Court of Quebec, Lesage, J.S.C.

September 8, 1995

An Act respecting the sovereignty of Québec (Draft Bill) – Agreement dated June 12, 1995 between the Parti Québécois, the Bloc Québécois and the Action démocratique du Québec — *An Act respecting the future of Québec* (Bill 1) introduced in the National Assembly of Québec on September 7, 1995 – Motion for provisional, interlocutory and permanent injunction and for a declaratory judgment against the Government of Québec.

The Plaintiff requested a declaratory judgment and a permanent injunction, as well as a provisional and interlocutory injunction against the Government of Québec.

He asserted that the conduct of the Government of Québec, as well as its acts with respect to the draft bill on the sovereignty of Québec and the agreement dated June 12, 1995 constitute an actual parliamentary and constitutional coup d'état, a fraud upon the Canadian Constitution and an abuse of powers, resulting in a violation and a denial of his rights and freedoms and those of all Québec taxpayers.

In particular, he asserted, among other claims, that the denial of his rights and freedoms and those of all Quebecers would result from the introduction by the Government of Québec, in the National Assembly, of a bill whose purpose is to allow the Government of Québec to unilaterally declare the independence of Québec after holding a referendum, without following the procedure set forth in the Canadian Constitution.

On the motion for a declaratory judgment, the Court ruled that it was in a position to grant such relief and declared that by introducing Bill 1, entitled *An act respecting the future of Québec*, whose purpose is to grant the National Assembly of Québec the power to proclaim that Québec has become a sovereign country, without being obliged to follow the amending formula provided for in Part v of the *Constitution Act, 1982*, the Government of Québec is:

- giving itself a mandate which is not conferred upon it by the Constitution of Canada and, in so doing, is acting beyond the powers granted to it by the Constitution;

- acting in such a manner as to repudiate the Constitution of Canada; and

- acting in violation of the constitutional order, such as to create serious and irreparable harm to the rights and freedoms of the Plaintiff and other Quebecers, contrary to the guarantees provided for in the *Canadian Charter of*

Rights and Freedoms, specifically in Sections 2, 3, 6, 7, 15 and 24(1).

On the matter of the injunction, the Court ruled that it would be preferable to let the public express its opinion in a referendum and that a declaratory judgment would be the appropriate remedy in the circumstances.

The Judgement of The Honorable Robert Lesage, J.S.C.

UNOFFICIAL TRANSLATION

CANADA

PROVINCE OF QUÉBEC   **SUPERIOR COURT**
DISTRICT OF QUÉBEC

No. 200-05-002117-955

QUÉBEC, September 8, 1995

PRESENT:—

THE HONORABLE ROBERT LESAGE, J.S.C.

GUY BERTRAND
attorney, practising at 1150 Claire-Fontaine, Suite 600, Québec, GIR 5G4

Plaintiff–petitioner

—v—

THE HONORABLE PAUL BÉGIN
in his capacity as Attorney General of Québec, 1200 Route de l'Église, 9th floor, Sainte-Foy, Québec

AND—

THE HONORABLE JACQUES PARIZEAU
in his capacity as Premier and Leader of the Government of Québec, 885 Grande-Allée East, 3rd floor, Building J, Québec, GIA IA2

AND—

ME PIERRE-F. CÔTÉ
in his capacity as Directeur général des élections et responsable des référendums pursuant to the Referendum Act, c. 64.1 of the Statutes of Québec, 3460 de la Pérade, Sainte-Foy, Québec, GIX 3Y5

Defendants–respondents

—AND—

THE HONORABLE DANIEL JOHNSON
in his capacity of Leader of the Official Opposition in the National Assembly, Hôtel du Parlement, Suite 2.83, Québec, GIA IA4

THE HONORABLE ALLAN ROCK
in his capacity of Attorney General of Canada, Justice Building, 239 Wellington Street, 3rd floor, Suite 360, Ottawa, Ontario, KIA OH8

THE HONORABLE EDMOND P. BLANCHARD
in his capacity of Attorney General of New Brunswick, Centennial Building, P.O. Box 6000, Fredericton, New Brunswick, B3B 5HI

THE HONORABLE J. WILLIAM GILLIS
in his capacity of Attorney General of Nova Scotia, 5151, Terminal Road, P.O. Box 7, Halifax, Nova Scotia, B3J 2L6

THE HONORABLE CLYDE K. WELLS
in his capacity of Attorney General of Newfoundland, Confederation Building, P.O. Box 8700, St. John's, Newfoundland, A1B 4J6

THE HONORABLE CHARLES HARNICK
in his capacity of Attorney General of Ontario, 720 Bay Street, 11th floor, Toronto, Ontario, M5G 2K1

THE HONORABLE ROSEMARY VODREY
in her capacity of Attorney General of Manitoba, 104 Legislative Building, Winnipeg, Manitoba, R3C 0V8

THE HONORABLE COLIN GABELMANN
in his capacity of Attorney General of British Columbia, Parliament Buildings, Suite 232, Victoria, British Columbia, V8V 1X4

THE HONORABLE ALAN G. BUCHANAN
in his capacity of Attorney General of Prince Edward Island, 11 Kent Street, 4th floor, P.O. Box 2000, Charlottetown, Prince Edward Island, C1A 7N8

THE HONORABLE NED SHILLINGTON
in his capacity of Attorney General of Saskatchewan, Legislative Building, Suite 355, Regina, Saskatchewan, S4S 0B3

THE HONORABLE BRIAN J. EVANS
in his capacity of Attorney General of Alberta, 320 Legislature Building, 10800, 97th Avenue, Edmonton, Alberta, T5K 2B6

THE HONORABLE DOUG PHILLIPS
in his capacity of Minister of Justice of the Yukon,
P.O. Box 2703, Whitehorse, Yukon, YIA 2C6

THE HONORABLE STEPHEN KAKFWI
in his capacity of Minister of Justice of the Northwest Territories, P.O. Box 1320, Yellowknife,
Northwest Territories, XIA 2L9

THE HONORABLE GHISLAIN PICARD
in his capacity of Regional Chief of the Assembly
of First Nations of Québec and Labrador

THE HONORABLE OVIDE MERCREDI
in his capacity of National Chief of the Assembly
of First Nations of Québec and Labrador

Intervenants

JUDGMENT

THE COURT was asked to grant interlocutory, declaratory and injunctive relief on the following matters:

THE MOTION

In one and the same procedural document attached to
the writ of summons, the Plaintiff asked for a declaratory
judgment and a permanent injunction (the action), as
well as a provisional and interlocutory injunction. The
[TRANSLATION] "conclusions sought on the motion for
provisional and interlocutory relief" are the same as those
sought in the action. The injunction was not granted on a
provisional basis when it was presented in chambers on
August 17, 1995.

The Plaintiff, whose standing in this matter was not contested, alleges in his declaration (paragraph 14) that [TRANSLATION] "the conduct of the Government of Québec, as well as its acts with respect to the draft sovereignty bill and the agreement of June 12, 1995, constitute an actual parliamentary and constitutional coup d'état, a fraud upon the Canadian Constitution and an abuse of powers, resulting in a violation and a denial of his rights and freedoms and those of all Québec taxpayers."

The draft bill on the sovereignty of Québec is a document which was tabled in the National Assembly by Premier Parizeau on December 6, 1994, together with a message addressed to each citizen of Québec asking him or her to [TRANSLATION] "examine, criticize or modify this draft bill as part of a vast process of democratic participation" and to "imagine together" the "declaration of sovereignty of Québec," which will serve as the preamble to the eventual bill.

The agreement of June 12, 1995 is an agreement between the representatives of the Parti québécois, the Bloc Québécois and the Action démocratique du Québec, three political parties, who have agreed upon a "common project to be submitted in the referendum" provided for in the draft bill. It refers to this referendum as the "Fall 1995 referendum" and it states that "the elements of this common project will be integrated in the bill that will be tabled in the Fall." The objective sought is described as follows:

"To achieve sovereignty for Québec and a formal proposal for a new economic and political partnership with Canada, aimed among other things at consolidating the existing economic space."

The conclusions for a declaratory judgment and for an injunction seek to obtain a remedy pursuant to the provisions of Section 24 of the Canadian Charter of Rights and Freedom; Subsection (1) reads as follows:

> **24.(1) [Enforcement of guaranteed rights and freedoms]** *Anyone whose rights or freedoms, as guaranteed by this Charter, have been infringed or denied may apply to a court of competent jurisdiction to obtain such remedy as the court considers appropriate and just in the circumstances."*

Every recourse is defined by its conclusions. In the present case, the conclusions in the motion, which are to be effective until a final judgment is rendered on the main action, cover over nine pages. In order to get a clear picture, it is therefore necessary to carry out an initial procedural analysis thereof.

The Plaintiff has divided his conclusions into two groups, namely:

(a)   30 judicial declarations which are sought from the Court;

(b)   20 requests for an injunction.

Not every judicial declaration has the effect of a declaratory judgment which acts as *res judicata* (a final judgment already decided between the parties). A declaratory judgment is usually found in the ruling, although the reasons for the ruling which are indissociable from it also constitute *res judicata*. The declaration which acts as *res judicata* is a ruling on a dispute between the parties. It is not simply a statement of the law, nor is it an opinion. However, the reasons state the opinion of the judge or judges hearing the case.

The conclusions drawn by the judge, both as to matters of fact and matters of law, are not declaratory judgments, unless, within the context of the case, they are stated so as to constitute *res judicata*. Several of the declarations sought by the Plaintiff are simply statements of law, theoretical declarations or judicial opinions. Others contemplate purely hypothetical situations. We shall ignore them for purposes of our examination.

Finally, those declarations with respect to matters of international law have no place here. While customary international law may be pleaded, it has no binding force, unless it is incorporated into the domestic law.

Putting aside the declaratory conclusions which, *prima facie* (on their face), cannot be ruled upon, there remain two types of declarations sought in the motion for inter-locutory relief, namely:

(a)   the declarations regarding the infringement of the fundamental rights of the Plaintiff;
(b)   the declarations whose purpose is to obtain a remedy for such an infringement.

The first ones are the following:

[TRANSLATION]

*"**DECLARE** that the Government of Quebec is seriously threatening the public order by preparing to use the powers of the National Assembly in order to destroy Canada by means of a unilateral declaration of independence as provided for in the draft sovereignty bill (P–1) and in the text of the agreement of June 12, 1995 (P–4), which would, for all practical purposes, amount to an actual constitutional and parliamentary coup d'état;*

***DECLARE** that the initiative of the Government of Québec, set forth in the draft sovereignty bill (P–1) and in the agreement of June 12, 1995 (P–4), results, for all practical purposes, in granting to Québec the right to secede from Canada;*

DECLARE that the attempt by the Premier of Québec and his Government, as set forth in the draft sovereignty bill (P–1) and in the agreement dated June 12, 1995 (P–4), to grant to the National Assembly the power to unilaterally separate Québec from the rest of Canada, after the holding of a referendum, seeks to partially or totally destroy the national unity and territorial integrity of Canada;

DECLARE that the Government of Québec is abusing its powers in order to obtain, by means of a bill (seeking the unilateral separation of Québec from Canada), the approval of the National Assembly in order to abolish the office of Lieutenant Governor and to modify the composition of the Supreme Court of Canada in contravention of the Canadian Constitution;

DECLARE that the Premier and his Government do not have the constitutional powers to table, before the National Assembly, a bill which essentially seeks the separation of Québec from Canada without having to comply with the process for amending the Constitution as provided for in Part V of the Constitution Act, 1982;

DECLARE that the draft sovereignty bill (P–1) and any similar bill (seeking the sovereignty of Québec in contravention of the Canadian Constitution and, in particular, in contravention of the amending formula provided for in the Constitution Act, 1982) threaten the rights and freedoms of the Plaintiff as guaranteed in Sections 2, 3, 6, 7, 15 and 24(1) of the Canadian Charter of Rights and Freedoms;

DECLARE that no law justifies such an infringement of the Plaintiff's rights and freedoms within such reasonable limits as can be demonstrably justified in a free and democratic society."

The declarations which seem to have been requested as a remedy are the following:

[TRANSLATION]

"DECLARE, contrary to what can be concluded from the text of the agreement of June 12, 1995 (P-4) and of the draft bill on the sovereignty of Québec (P-1)), that the National Assembly of Québec does not have the capacity nor the power to unilaterally declare the sovereignty of Québec, without being obliged to follow the amending formula provided for in the Canadian Constitution;

DECLARE that the Government of Quebec is acting in contravention of the law by preparing to put everything into place in order to use its majority in the National Assembly in order to force the latter to adopt a bill whose purpose is to destroy Canada by means of a unilateral declaration of independence;

DECLARE that the National Assembly of Québec does not have the power to modify the powers of the Lieutenant Governor to assent to a law;

DECLARE that the referendum provided for in the draft sovereignty bill (P-1) or in the agreement of June 12, 1995 (P-4) is ultra vires (beyond) the powers of the National Assembly since it seeks to have the sovereignty bill approved by means of a referendum, thereby creating an intermediary between the National Assembly and the Lieutenant Governor of Québec;

DECLARE that the referendum provided for in the draft bill (P-1) and the referendum provided for in the agreement of June 12, 1995 (P-4) is ultra vires the powers of the National Assembly, to the extent that they seek to have the citizens approve a bill which is, on its face, unconstitutional;

DECLARE that the Government of Québec cannot issue an order in council ordering the Directeur général des élections to hold the referendum provided for in the draft sovereignty bill (P–1) and in the agreement of June 12, 1995 (P–4);

DECLARE that the Government of Québec cannot use public funds in order to carry out the referendum contemplated in sections 16 and 17 of its draft bill or the referendum contemplated on page 2 [page 1 of the English version] of the agreement of June 12, 1995 (P–4);

DECLARE that any bill which reiterates the provisions of the agreement ratified and signed on June 12, 1995 by Messrs. Jacques Parizeau, Lucien Bouchard and Mario Dumont (P–4), whose purpose is to grant the National Assembly of Québec the capacity or the power to declare the sovereignty of Quebec, without being obliged to follow the amending procedure provided for in Part V of the Constitution Act, 1982, would constitute a serious threat to the rights and freedoms of the Plaintiff as guaranteed by the Canadian Charter of Rights and Freedoms, in particular, by Sections 2, 3, 6, 7, 15 and 24(1);

DECLARE that the Respondent, Pierre-F. Côté, the Directeur général des élections, does not have the power to hold a referendum on a bill whose purpose is to directly or indirectly authorize the National Assembly to unilaterally declare the sovereignty of Québec and, in particular, to declare the sovereignty of Québec without having to obtain the consent of seven Canadian provinces having fifty per cent of the population, or the unanimous consent of the provinces, as well as the consent of the Senate and of the House of Commons in order to abolish the office of Lieutenant Governor and to modify the Supreme Court of Canada;

DECLARE, given the rare and exceptional circumstances of this case, that the Plaintiff is entitled to obtain from the Attorney General of Québec all costs relating to the present proceedings, including experts' fees, if necessary, and payment of all lawyers' fees on the same basis as those which are paid to lawyers in private practice who are hired by the Government of Québec pursuant to orders in council to that effect;"

The conclusions requesting injunctions are all meant to obtain a remedy or to enforce the respect of the rights and freedoms of the Plaintiff as guaranteed by the Canadian Charter of Rights and Freedoms. They read as follows:

[TRANSLATION]

"The rights and freedoms of the Plaintiff

ENJOIN the Defendants, the Attorney General of Québec, Mr. Paul Bégin, the Premier of Québec, Mr. Jacques Parizeau, and all members of the Government of Québec to cease threatening to jeopardize the rights and freedoms of the Plaintiff and of Québec taxpayers as guaranteed by Sections 2, 3, 6, 7, 15 and 24 of the Canadian Charter of Rights and Freedoms, by using the powers of the National Assembly, which is composed of a majority of members of the Parti québécois, in order to adopt a bill whose purpose is, without question, to amend the Constitution of Canada without obtaining the consent of the other Canadian partners, as provided for in Part V of the Constitution Act, 1982;

Bill on unilateral sovereignty

ENJOIN the Defendants and all members of the Government of Québec to stop the process provided for in the draft sovereignty bill (P–1) and in the agreement of June 12, 1995

(P–4) whose purpose is to use the powers of the National Assembly of Québec in order to enable the latter to declare the sovereignty of Québec without being obliged to use the procedure provided for in Part V of the Constitutional Act, 1982 and, in particular, to take all the necessary measures:

(a)   In order not to table before the National Assembly of Québec a bill on the sovereignty of Québec whose purpose is to grant it the powers to destroy Canada by means of a unilateral declaration of independence or, more specifically, without having to follow the amending process provided for in the Canadian Constitution;

(b)   In order to withdraw from the National Assembly the draft bill on the sovereignty of Québec (P–1) tabled on December 6, 1994 by the Defendant, Premier Jacques Parizeau;

(c)   To see to it that the draft bill on the sovereignty of Québec (P–1) or any similar bill resulting from the text of the agreement signed on June 12, 1995 (exhibit P–4) between the Parti québécois, the Bloc Québécois and the Action démocratique du Québec (whose purpose is to provide the National Assembly with the capacity or the power to declare the sovereignty of Québec, without the consent of the rest of Canada, as is required by the Canadian Constitution) is not introduced to the National Assembly of Québec in order that it be discussed and/or adopted in accordance with the Act respecting the National Assembly and the relevant regulations;

(d)   In order that no bill authorizing the National Assembly of Québec to unilaterally declare the sovereignty of Québec, without the consent of the rest of Canada, be submitted for the approval of the citizens by means of a referendum;

(e)   In order that no question whose purpose is to authorize the National Assembly to declare the sovereignty of Québec in contravention of the Canadian Constitution be submitted to the citizens by means of a referendum;

(f)   In order not to use the powers of the National Assembly of Québec for the purpose of proceeding with the separation of Québec from Canada without the consent of the federal Parliament, the Senate and the other Canadian legislatures, as required by Part V of the Constitution Act, 1982;

The paramountcy of the Constitution and democracy

ENJOIN the Attorney General of Québec, the Premier, Mr. Jacques Parizeau, and all members of the Government of Québec, not to put into use or exercise any of the rights which they claim to hold pursuant to a bill on the sovereignty of Québec, to the extent that this act seeks the separation of Québec from the rest of Canada in a manner which is not in compliance with the Canadian Constitution;

ORDER the Attorney General of Québec, the Premier, Mr. Jacques Parizeau, and all members of the Government of Québec to stop placing themselves outside the law, within the scope of the realization of the sovereignty plan provided for in the draft bill on the sovereignty of Québec (P–1);

ENJOIN the Attorney General of Québec, the Premier, Mr. Jacques Parizeau, and all members of his Government to comply with the provisions prescribed by the Canadian Constitution, in particular, with the Constitution Act, 1867 and the Constitution Act, 1982;

ORDER *the Attorney General of Québec, the Premier, Mr. Jacques Parizeau, and all members of the Government of Québec to stop preparing any forcible parliamentary or constitutional takeover by drafting a bill which would grant the national Assembly the power to declare the sovereignty of Québec when it deems it advisable and without being obliged to follow the amending process provided for in Part V of the Constitution Act, 1982;*

Referendum and public funds

ORDER *the Defendants and all members of the Government of Québec not to issue any order in council ordering the Directeur general des élections to hold the referendum provided for in the draft sovereignty bill (P–1) and in the agreement of June 12, 1995 (P–4);*

ENJOIN *the Attorney General of Québec, the Premier, Mr. Jacques Parizeau, and all members of the Government of Québec not to use public funds in order to carry out the referendum provided for in sections 16 and 17 of the draft sovereignty bill (P–1) or the referendum provided for in the agreement of June 12, 1995 (P–4), or any other referendum whose purpose is to destroy the Canadian Constitution other than by following the amending process provided for therein;*

ENJOIN *the Attorney General of Québec, the Premier, Mr. Jacques Parizeau, and all members of the Government of Québec not to use public funds for purpose of propaganda and publicity seeking to destroy the Canadian Constitution or to withdraw Québec from Canada other than by complying with the provisions set forth in Part V of the Constitution Act, 1982;*

ENJOIN *the Attorney General of Québec, the Premier, Mr. Jacques Parizeau, and all members of the Government* *of Québec not to pay any public monies into the referendum fund in order to carry out the public consultation provided for in the draft sovereignty bill (P–1) or the referendum provided for in the agreement of June 12,1995 (P–4), or any other referendum whose purpose is to give a mandate to the National Assembly to unilaterally declare the sovereignty of Québec in contravention of Part V of the Constitution Act, 1982;*

The Directeur général des élections

ENJOIN the Defendant, Mr. Pierre-F. Côté, in his capacity as Directeur général des élections:

(a) Not to hold the referendum provided for in sections 16 and 17 of the draft sovereignty bill (P–1), nor the referendum provided for in the agreement of June 12, 1995 (P–4), nor any referendum whatsoever whose purpose is to give the National Assembly a mandate to declare the sovereignty of Québec without the consent of the rest of Canada, as required by the provisions of Part V of the Constitution Act, 1982;

(b) To avoid incurring any public expenses or spending any public funds whatsoever in order to carry out the referendum;

(c) Not to give effect to the order in council which the Government may send to him ordering him to hold the referendum provided for in the draft sovereignty bill (P–1) and/or in the agreement of June 12, 1995 (P–4), or any referendum whose purpose is to directly or indirectly authorize the National Assembly to unilaterally declare the sovereignty of Québec and, in particular, to declare the sovereignty of Québec without having to obtain the consent of seven Canadian

provinces having fifty per cent of the population, or the unanimous consent of the provinces, as well as the consent of the Senate and of the House of Commons in order to abolish the office of Lieutenant Governor and to modify the Supreme Court of Canada;

(d) Not to deliver a copy of the Government order in council to the Returning officer in any of the electoral districts of Québec;

Fees and expenses

ORDER the Attorney General of Québec to pay all costs, including experts' fees and the fees of all professionals which the Plaintiff has been obliged to retain or will be obliged to retain with respect to the present litigation, on the same basis as that used by the Government of Québec when it retains the services of lawyers in private practice, the whole in accordance with the Government's order in council to that effect;"

APPEARANCES

None of the Intervenants filed an appearance. The Defendants were represented, but after four days of a hearing on a motion by the Attorney General to decline the jurisdiction of the Court and the Court's decision to continue to hear the case, the attorneys of the Defendant Paul Bégin, in his capacity as Attorney General, and of the Defendant Parizeau, in his capacity as Premier and Leader of the Government of Quebec, declared that they were withdrawing on instructions of their clients, at the same time as a meeting of Cabinet was announced with respect to the present proceedings.

The attorneys of the Defendants Parizeau and Bégin, in their respective capacities, justified their attitude by stating:

[TRANSLATION]

"As we have pleaded over the last few days, the Attorney General considers that the right of the National Assembly to debate the referendum process is at the very core of its privileges. The Government reiterates the rights of Quebecers to pronounce themselves on their future within the scope of a referendum held in accordance with the Referendum Act."

Leaving aside any substantive questions, it should be noted, at this point, that neither the National Assembly nor its speaker is a party to these proceedings. The opinion issued in 1965 by Louis-Philippe Pigeon, an eminent jurist who was then legal counsel for the Government, an opinion relied upon by the Defendants, dealt with a very different matter. Gabias, a member of the National Assembly had instituted proceedings against the National Assembly who was impleaded as a party.

Thus, the inquiry regarding the interlocutory measures took place in the absence of the Government's attorneys. The Defendant Pierre-F. Côté, in his capacity as Directeur général des élections, continued to be represented by attorneys. The Defendant filed no evidence. For his part, the Plaintiff, who is relying on his affidavit in support of his motion, testified before the Court. No objection was raised to this evidence.

PARLIAMENTARY PRIVILEGE

To our surprise, the attorneys for the Defendants Bégin and Parizeau stated that they had no other claims than those raised in the motion "to dismiss" filed by the Attorney

General, i.e. that the present recourse is not within the jurisdiction of the courts. In this motion "to dismiss," the assertion is stated as follows:

[TRANSLATION]

5. Through the conclusions sought, the petitioner is asking the Court to interfere with the exercise of legislative powers and with the workings of the National Assembly; this would constitute an unjustifiable attack on the fundamental powers of the National Assembly, as well as on its most essential privileges; "

In reality, the motion "to dismiss" contains a second argument with respect to the request for an injunction against the holding of the Fall 1995 referendum; it reads as follows:

[TRANSLATION]

"13. The holding of the referendum in question is based on the principle of democracy and it deals with an issue which does not fall within the jurisdiction of the courts;"

In these proceedings, the Government is a party, not the National Assembly. Parliamentary privileges are relevant only as regards measures which are requested in order to remedy a violation of the Canadian Charter of Rights and Freedoms. We must conclude that the Attorney General is leaving it up to justice as regards the violation of the fundamental rights and freedoms of the Plaintiff, since he has not taken a position as regards this matter.

The key decision as regards parliamentary privilege is that rendered by the Supreme Court of Canada in *N.B. Broadcasting Co. v. N.S. ([1993] 1 S.C.R. 319)*. The Court was divided on the constitutional nature of parliamentary privileges and on the application of the Charter to a legislative assembly. The majority concluded that "the privilege of the legislative assembly to exclude strangers enjoys constitutional status as part of the Constitution of Canada, and hence cannot be abrogated by another part of the Constitution," i.e. the freedom of expression provided for in the Charter of Rights and Freedoms.

The judges were unanimous in recognizing the right of the courts to examine the existence and extent of the privilege, but not its exercise (per Lamer, C.J., p. 350; per McLachlin, J., p. 382). They also agreed that the parliamentary privileges of the British Parliament at Westminster were not carried over as whole to Canada (per Lamer, C.J., p. 343; per McLachlin, J., p. 380).

Mrs. Justice McLachlin, who was in the majority, cited the work of professor Dawson and Joseph Maingot [sic] (p. 380) and referred to the notion of parliamentary privilege as being a very restricted power which is necessary to maintain order and discipline in the exercise of the functions of the members of the Assembly. She noted that Maingot [sic] includes within these privileges, freedom of expression of the members of the Assembly and the necessary powers to protect and defend them. Immunity is the corollary of privilege. Justice McLachlin concludes as follows (p. 384):

> *"In summary, it seems clear that, from an historical perspective, Canadian legislative bodies possess such inherent privileges as may be necessary for their proper functioning. These privileges are part of the fundamental law and hence are constitutional. The courts may determine if the privilege claimed is necessary to the capacity of the legislature to function, but have no power to review the rightness or wrongness of a particular decision made pursuant to the privilege."*

Among the unwritten and inherent constitutional privileges of our legislative bodies, the Supreme Court, under the hand of Justice McLachlin, recognized (pp. 385 and 386) freedom of expression in the Assembly, the right of the Assembly to be the sole judge of the lawfulness of its proceedings, the right to expel any outsider from the gallery and the right to control the publication of the debates.

In giving precedence to the inherent privileges of the Canadian legislative bodies over the entrenchment of the written rights guaranteed by the Charter, Justice McLachlin adds that this is not "a mere convention to which the courts have not given legal effect" (p. 377).

From the decision of *N.B. Broadcasting* one must retain the point that parliamentary privileges are intended to ensure the operation of the legislative bodies and not that of the executive branch, that these privileges exist only to the extent that this type of immunity is necessary for the exercise of legislative functions and that they are constitutional principles, in the same manner as the Charter of Rights and Freedoms, and that they cannot be frustrated by the Charter.

The draft sovereignty bill is not an act of the National Assembly. It is not a bill tabled for a first reading, but rather a governmental document of a political nature. Parliamentary privilege cannot be invoked with respect to it, since this privilege does not belong to the Government, but rather to the National Assembly. The same can be said of orders in council adopted by the Government for putting into place the sovereignty commissions and for the spending, by the Government, of public funds for this process.

On the other hand, in choosing the remedies for the infringement of rights and freedoms, it is clear that the Court cannot violate the parliamentary privileges of the National Assembly and those of its members.

Beyond parliamentary privileges, the Court recognizes that the executive and legislative branches, on the one hand, and the judicial branch, on the other hand, have traditionally enjoyed their own autonomy in the manner in which their business is conducted. The attitude of each of them towards the other, of not interfering with their powers, is a usage, if not a convention which enables our democratic system to function within the rule of law.

NATURE OF THE RECOURSE

The action commenced by the Plaintiff is not an action for an act carried out by the Government nor a request that the Court invalidate the provisions of a particular law pursuant to subsection (1) of section 52 of the Constitution Act, 1982. It is a separate recourse, under section 24, in order to obtain a remedy which is "appropriate and just in the circumstances" for the denial of the Plaintiff's rights and freedoms as guaranteed by the Canadian Charter of Rights and Freedoms.

The criteria which a court must consider in matters of interlocutory injunctions are those which must guide us in this case, even if the interlocutory measures requested are both requested by means of a judicial declaration and an injunction. They are the same as those applied in stays of proceedings. They were set out by Mr. Justice Beetz in the decision of *Manitoba (A.G.) v. Metropolitan Stores Ltd.* (*[1987] 1 S.C.R. 110*). Recently, the Supreme Court of Canada dealt with this matter once again in *RJR–MacDonald Inc. v. Canada (A.G.) ([1994] 1 S.C.R. 311)*. The three criteria which were already cited in *Metropolitan Stores* were considered once against with respect to a request for relief from the application of a regulation, where the Charter of Rights and

Freedoms and the public interest were pleaded. (The case dealt with a request for relief from the application of certain provisions of the Tobacco Products Control Regulations, while the enabling act, The Tobacco Products Control Act, was the subject of a contestation before the Court.) These criteria are seen as three stages which the court will follow in its analysis of the interlocutory request, namely:

1- Establish whether there is a serious question to be tried, by carrying out a limited review of the matter, or by carrying out a more detailed analysis where the interlocutory remedy is equivalent, in fact, to a final determination of the action, or where the issue at hand is a pure question of constitutional law. In this last event, which is an extremely rare case, the interlocutory remedy may be granted without proceeding with an analysis under the second and third stages.

2- The second stage consists of determining whether there will be irreparable harm if the relief is not granted.

3- The third stage consists of weighing the balance of inconvenience between the parties, taking the public interest into account.

THE EVIDENCE

The Plaintiff's affidavit and his testimony during the hearings are not contested. Of course, the Court must make a distinction between a statement of fact and the analysis thereof which the Plaintiff may have made in his statements.

The Plaintiff decided to institute the present proceedings after the tabling, on December 6, 1994, of a draft bill on the sovereignty of Québec by Premier Parizeau on behalf of the Government of Québec. The first section of this draft bill states:

"1. Québec is a sovereign country."

The draft bill is preceded by explanatory notes indicating that this is a political course of action put forth by the Government of Québec. The project is described as follows:

"It is proposed that Québec become a sovereign country through the democratic process. The accession to full sovereignty has been defined by the National Assembly as 'the accession of Québec to a position of exclusive jurisdiction, through its democratic institutions, to make laws and levy taxes in its territory and to act on the international scene for the making of agreements and treaties of any kind with other independent States and participating in various international organizations.'

---

1 — Act respecting the process for determining the political and constitutional future of Québec (S. Q., 1991, c. 34).

An economic association with Canada would be maintained in order to preserve and further develop the free circulation of goods and services, of capital and of persons that is currently prevailing. To the same end, Québec would continue to adhere to the North American Free Trade Agreement and the General Agreement on Tariffs and Trade. The Canadian dollar would continue to be the legal currency of Québec.

A new constitution would be drafted following a procedure to be defined by the National Assembly. This new constitution would include a charter of human rights and freedoms and provide guarantees, in a manner consistent with Québec's territorial integrity, to the English-speaking community and to the Aboriginal nations. It would also provide for the decentralization of specific powers to local and regional authorities, together with sufficient resources.

Provisions are made as to the territory of a sovereign Québec, Québec citizenship and the continuity of treaties, international alliances and laws. In this respect, the Government of Québec would be authorized to take over, from the Government of Canada, all services and transfer payments currently provided to Québec citizens by the Canadian government.

Several other transitional measures are provided for, including the conclusion of an agreement on the apportionment of the property and debts of Canada."

The explanatory notes also set forth the process which the Government intends to follow in order to make Québec a separate country. This process consists of six steps described as follows:

"*1-*   *publication of the draft bill;*

2-   *a period of information and participation for the purposes of improving the bill and drafting the 'Declaration of Sovereignty' which will form the preamble to the bill;*

3-   *discussion of the bill respecting the sovereignty of Québec, and passage by the National Assembly;*

4-   *approval of the Act by the population in a referendum;*

5-   *a period of discussions with Canada on the transitional measures to be set in place, particularly as regards the apportionment of property and debts; during this period the new Québec constitution will be drafted;*

6-   *the accession of Québec to sovereignty."*

The first two steps have already been completed or are in the process of being completed. Orders in council were adopted in January and February 1995 in order to create various regional commissions "on the future of Québec" and two commissions addressing the elderly and the young, the whole under the auspices of a "national" commission of which the Premier is a member.

The Plaintiff alleges that according to information in his possession $5,000,000 of public funds have already been spent in order to implement and operate these commissions and that several thousand dollars have been spent to have studies carried out on the sovereignty of Québec and to disseminate propaganda in support of this option.

The Plaintiff appeared before one of these commissions. He stated that the Official Opposition refuses to participate in these commissions on sovereignty because it considers them to be "fake".

The National Commission on the Future of Québec issued its report to the Premier on April 19, 1995. On June 12, 1995, an agreement was entered into between the Premier, representing the Parti québécois, Lucien Bouchard, representing the Bloc Québécois, and Mario Dumont, representing the Action démocratique du Québec; this is the agreement referred to at the beginning of this judgment and whose parameters are to be integrated into the announced bill.

The Plaintiff claims that the acts of the Government and all costs incurred and paid from public funds in order to effect the secession of Québec are illegal, since they fall within the scope of a project which proposes, in violation of the Constitution of Canada, [TRANSLATION] "to separate Québec from Canada without having to comply with the amending formula provided for in the Constitution Act, 1982." He states that the Government of Québec is acting against the public order and in an anarchistic manner by placing itself outside the supreme law of the country, that it is preparing to use its majority in the National Assembly in order to carry out an actual constitutional coup d'état, in which it is involving the public without informing it of the violation of the Constitution. He alleges that the Defendants are acting in bad faith and compares their acts to a conspiracy against the State. He qualifies the process undertaken by the Government of Québec as a constitutional revolution which is not justified by international law.

The Plaintiff has asked the Court, as guardian of the Constitution, to protect his rights and freedoms which are seriously threatened by the [TRANSLATION] "strategy and the actions of the Government of Québec as embodied in the draft bill on the sovereignty of Québec and in the text of the agreement between the Parti québécois, the Bloc Québécois and the Action démocratique du Québec" (paragraph 102 of the declaration). He claims that the Government of Québec is seriously threatening the public order rather than governing in accordance with the rule of law.

In his testimony before the Court, the Plaintiff bolstered the allegations contained in the declaration to the effect that the rights and freedoms guaranteed to him by the Canadian Charter of Rights and Freedoms are seriously threatened, namely:

- his freedom of thought, opinion and expression, as determined and applied by the Canadian courts, particularly by the Supreme Court of Canada;

- his Canadian citizenship, his right to vote and to run for office in federal elections;

- his right to enter, remain in and leave Canada as he pleases;

- his right to move to and take up residence throughout the country and to pursue the gaining of a livelihood therein;

- his right to liberty and to the security of the person in the event of a disruption in the legal system;

- his right to be treated equally and without discrimination with respect to other Canadians;

- his right to have recourse to the Canadian Charter of Rights and Freedoms and to its interpretation by the Supreme Court of Canada in order to obtain a remedy in the event of an infringement, which would prevent him from exercising even the present recourse.

He strongly alleges that once sovereignty is declared, he will have lost the assistance of the court to protect his fundamental rights and freedoms.

The Plaintiff declares that he is acting not only on his own behalf, but also on behalf of millions of Quebecers.

In fact, the Plaintiff's situation is no different than that of other Quebecers, which does not mean that he may not seek the protection of the courts to have the rights and freedoms guaranteed to him by the Constitution respected. This is the basis of his recourse.

On the other hand, the position maintained by the Government and which underlies the representations made by its attorneys, is that the democratic principle of the referendum is applicable in this case. Before drawing any conclusions, we believe it would be useful to review certain principles of constitutional law.

SOME PRINCIPLES

The political set-up of a society draws on the sociological and historical background of the nation. The State is born out of its political set-up. Every state does not necessarily exercise full sovereignty over its territory and the people who inhabit it. The provinces in our federal regime are an example, as in every federation. International recognition is a factor to be considered in determining the sovereignty of a country.

The constitution of a sovereign country, that is, the group of rules which govern the institutions constituting its political structure, is not always written. The constitution is not an act, in the sense that it does not emanate from the legislative branch of the country, even if it may take the form of an act. It cannot depend upon an act. To the contrary, acts must respect the constitution. That is why the Constitution of Canada is defined as "the supreme law of Canada" in the Constitution Act, 1982 (s. 52).

The legal system is a manifestation of the sovereignty of the State, which must ensure the allegiance of judges. The judicial branch exists in societies which recognize the paramountcy of the law, in order to have the rule of law respected and, most importantly, to have the acts adopted by the legislative branch respected. In a federal system, the legal system includes rules which establish the distribution of powers between the central state and the federated states. These rules may be enforced by the courts.

The judicial branch does not create the law, even less the constitution by which it is created. It interprets them. In this regard, it is different from the executive branch, namely the Government, which is the only body entrusted with the duty and the responsibility to act in the name of the State. The role of the judicial branch is circumscribed by the legal rules in place, which are usually found in legislation. Now, it is recognized that certain constitutional usages, called conventions, are rules which are not enforceable by the courts (Re: Resolution to amend the Constitution, [1981] 1

S.C.R. 753). In contrast with conventions, a coup d'état or a revolution can occur, resulting in a breach of the legal system about which the courts can do nothing.

In fact, the sovereignty of a country results from the *de facto* exercise of authority over a territory and the people who inhabit it. This exercise of authority is ensured by the voluntary or forced acceptance of the rules which govern the relations between the State and the citizens, including the constitution. These rules may be amended in accordance with the procedure provided for in the existing legal system, i.e. by acting within the bounds of the law, but they may be amended by means of an entity which places itself above the existing constitution and which has the physical control of the territory and the acceptance of the population which inhabits it.

This last method is not legal. A new legal system can arise only after a fait accompli. This situation was seen in Southern Rhodesia. Professor Peter Hogg described this as follows in his textbook entitled CONSTITUTIONAL LAW OF CANADA (2nd edition, p. 104):

> *"In assessing the legality of a regime established by revolution — meaning any break in legal continuity — the issue for the courts is simply whether or not the revolution has been successful. As de Smith says, 'legal theorists have no option but to accommodate their concepts to the facts of political life'[115] In* Madzimbamuto v. Lardner-Burke *(1969),[116] the Privy Council had to decide whether validity should be accorded to the acts of the legislature and government of Southern Rhodesia after the 'unilateral declaration of independence' (U.D.I.) from Britain. Their lordships held that the post-U.D.I. acts were not valid, because it could not be said 'with certainty' that the break-away government was in effective control of the territory which*

it claimed the right to govern. Their lordships pointed out that Britain was still claiming to be the lawful government and was taking steps to regain control. In a later case, the Appellate Division of the High Court of Rhodesia decided that, having regard to developments since the decision of Madzimbamuto, *it could 'now predict with certainty that sanctions will not succeed in their objective of overthrowing the present government and of restoring the British government to the control of the government of Rhodesia.'[117] The Court accordingly held that the existing Rhodesian government was the legal government, and the post-U.D.I. constitution was the only valid constitution."[118]*

---

115 de Smith, 76.

116 [1969] 1 A.C. 645.

117 R. v. Ndhlovu [1968] 4 S.A.L.R. 515, 532. The decision was never appealed to the Privy Council, probably because the Rhodesian government did not recognize the authority of the Privy Council (the government was not represented before the Privy Council in Madzimbamuto) and an appeal would have been futile.

118 Subsequent events suggested that this conclusion was premature. Guerilla war led the break-away government to seek a constitutional settlement with the United Kingdom (as well as with the blacks of Southern Rhodesia). A settlement was agreed upon at a conference in London in 1979, and independence and a new constitution (under which the white minority no longer held power) was granted to the state, now called Zimbabwe, by imperial statute: Zimbabwe Act 1979 (U.K.), c. 60; Zimbabwe Constitution Order 1979 (U.K.), S.I. 1979, No. 1600.

In the decision of *Blackburn v. Attorney General ([1971] 2 All ER 1380)*, issued by the Privy Council with respect to an attempt to block the negotiations regarding the entry of the

United Kingdom into the common European Market, a decision which is referred to by the Supreme Court of Canada in the reference on the patriation (Re: Resolution to amend the Constitution, [1981] 1 S.C.R. 753), Lord Denning Mr., of the United Kingdom Court of Appeal, after indicating that the courts may not interfere with the negotiation of international treaties, cited with approval an article written by Professor H.W.R. Wade and published in the Cambridge Law Journal ([1954–55] CLJ p. 196), where it is stated that: "Sovereignty is a political fact for which no purely legal authority can be constituted."

We should add here that the decision of the British Court of Appeal was based on the supremacy of Parliament, which has no limits in the United Kingdom's unitary system, while in Canada sovereignty is shared between the federal authority and the provinces, and is subject to the interpretation of the courts.

THE DISPUTED CLAIMS

Firstly, we are asked to evaluate the right claimed by the Plaintiff, namely, whether the acts of the Government threaten the rights and freedoms which are guaranteed to him by the Canadian Charter of Rights and Freedoms. The Charter, which was introduced by the Constitution Act, 1982, is part of the Constitution of Canada. There can be no question that it applies to Québec. The Supreme Court of Canada clearly expressed this fact in *Quebec Constitutional Amendment Reference (No. 2), ([1982] 45 N.R. 317, 331)*:

"The Constitution Act, 1982 is now in force. Its legality is neither challenged nor assailable. It contains a new procedure for amending the Constitution of Canada which entirely replaces the old one in its legal as well as in its

conventional aspects. Even assuming therefore that there was a conventional requirement for the consent of Quebec under the old system, it would no longer have any object or force."

In no way can the legitimization or the forced imposition of a new legal system be considered as a possibility which the Court should take into account.

The paramountcy of the law is recognized by the Constitution of Canada (preamble to the Canadian Charter of Rights and Freedoms) and our higher courts have often confirmed that the courts are the guardians of the Constitution. We are aware of no authority to the contrary.

The recourse provided for in section 24(1) to obtain a remedy is the appropriate recourse when there is a violation of the rights and freedoms guaranteed by the Charter (B.C.G.E.U. v. British Columbia (A.G.), [1988] 2 S.C.R. 214, 230). The Charter applies not only to the Parliament and Government of Canada in respect of all matters within the authority of Parliament, but also to the legislature and government of each province in respect of all matters within the authority of this legislature (s. 32 of the Constitution Act, 1982). The Court cannot accept, as was suggested, that governmental actions which do not create obligations are not subject to the control of the courts pursuant to the Charter. This would result in limiting the application of the Charter to rules of law, which may be declared to be of no force or effect pursuant to section 52 of the Constitution Act, 1982. The Charter applies to any act on the part of the government if the government's actions violate the rights and freedoms guaranteed by it.

The Premier is a member of, and the chairperson of the Executive Council (s. 6, Executive Power Act, c. E–18) which, together with the Lieutenant Governor, forms the

Government of Québec. When Premier Parizeau announced the draft bill, he acted as Premier, as appears from this draft bill and from the message signed by the Premier himself and annexed thereto. The orders in council adopted in January and February 1995, regarding the commissions on the future of Québec, were adopted in the name of the Government and indicate that the Government tabled a draft bill on the sovereignty of Québec in the National Assembly.

Order in council 1–95 dated January 11, 1995, "regarding the commissions on the future of Québec," gives to the commissions the mandate to hear the testimony of individuals and groups wishing to express themselves and, in particular, it states that they are responsible for "receiving suggestions from individuals concerning the writing of a Declaration of Sovereignty to be included in the preamble of proposed legislation respecting Québec sovereignty." This process has already commenced; public funds have been expended and the Government is preparing to initiate the referendum process.

The actions of the Government of Québec and the process set forth in the draft bill show that the Government, through the Premier and other cabinet ministers, has undertaken on behalf of Québec, to proceed with a unilateral declaration of independence and to have Québec recognized as a state separate from the rest of Canada.

It is evident, if not expressly stated, that the Government of Québec does not intend to comply with the amending formula contained in the Constitution in order to carry out the secession of Québec. In this regard, the Government of Québec is giving itself a mandate which is not conferred upon it by the Constitution of Canada.

The actions of the Government of Québec to achieve the secession of Québec are a repudiation of the Constitution of Canada. If such an event were to occur, the Canadian Charter of Rights and Freedoms, which is part of the Constitution of Canada, would cease to apply to Québec and the Plaintiff would be unable to demand that it be respected.

It is not our place to judge the probability that the Government's objective will be realized. It is sufficient for us to recognize that its actions are affecting the political institutions of Canada at their very roots and are denying to the Plaintiff Bertrand, as well as to the other citizens of Québec, the protection afforded to them by the Constitution of Canada with regard to the respect of their fundamental rights and freedoms. The promise to substitute a charter of individual rights and freedoms in a future constitution is not the equivalent of the constitutional guarantee which each Canadian now has.

The constitutional change proposed by the Government of Québec would entail a break in the legal system which is manifestly contrary to the Constitution of Canada. It does not follow that the various measures requested by the Plaintiff in the numerous conclusions of his motion must be granted. It must be remembered that the Charter guarantees the fundamental rights and freedoms and not the remedies (R. v. Rahey, [1987] 1 S.C.R. 588). However, the clearly illegal actions of the Government lead us to conclude that the Plaintiff is entitled to a remedy which the Court considers "appropriate and just in the circumstances." This remedy will ultimately have to be determined by the judge who hears the action on its merits.

IRREPARABLE INJURY

The Plaintiff claims that in the event of an affirmative vote in the referendum, he will have lost the protection of the rights and freedoms guaranteed to him by the Canadian Charter. At the same time, he predicts there will be chaos in the legal system, resulting in the duty of the federal Government to defend the citizens of Québec who do not want to accept the new legal system. These two statements are, at the very least, contradictory.

The Court cannot prevent the exercise of political forces. On the other hand, the Court cannot approve of a violation of the constitutional system. The process implemented by the Government of Québec may lead to such a violation. This is not mere speculation. The Government has taken major steps to achieve its ends. It is seeking to change the constitutional system by using its political powers and public funds. The Plaintiff opposes this process. The tension under which he and the other citizens are living can only worsen from day to day. The threat is a serious one. The same can be said of public order. The harm will be irreparable.

BALANCE OF INCONVENIENCE

The Plaintiff is asking us, at the interlocutory stage, to grant all of the remedies sought. Among these remedies, the injunction against the holding of the referendum has blown this case out of proportion. From a simple court action, one is asked to conclude that the courts may interfere with the affairs of the National Assembly.

A referendum, by its nature, is a consultative process (Haig v. Canada, [1993] 2 S.C.R. 995, 1032). It does not offend the legal or constitutional system. The Plaintiff has made many declarations to the effect that he is not opposed to the holding of a purely consultative referendum. The problem is the effect that would result from a law such as the draft bill presented by the Government, upon the approval, by means of a referendum, of a declaration of sovereignty.

It contemplates the implementation of a new legal system and a transitional period during which negotiations would be undertaken with the rest of Canada. Concurrently, measures would be taken for the adoption of a new constitution for Québec.

We take judicial notice (art. 2808 C.C.Q.) of Bill 1 of the 35th legislature, entitled AN ACT RESPECTING THE FUTURE OF QUÉBEC, which was introduced on September 7, 1995 and which states (s. 6) that a constituent commission will be established to draw up a draft of a new constitution. This new constitution would then be submitted to another referendum. In the interim, which is of an indefinite duration, a transitional constitution would be adopted by the Parliament of Québec. Section 26 authorizes the National Assembly to proclaim sovereignty at any time after the law has been assented to, if, in the opinion of an orientation and supervision committee responsible for negotiating with the Government of Canada, these negotiations fail.

In such a case, the stability of the legal system would be compromised. The balance of inconvenience undoubtedly requires that, in the public interest, the Court provide a remedy now which is practical and effective.

Parliamentary privilege cannot place the National Assembly above the Constitution of Canada. The members may discuss any subject and adopt any measures they wish, even if they are invalid and illegal, but there is a limit; they cannot attack the very Constitution from which they draw their powers. In cases brought before them, the courts must denounce unconstitutional measures.

The National Assembly of Québec does not have the powers of the Parliament at Westminster. In the Privy Council decision of *Rediffusion (Hong Kong) Ltd. v. Attorney General of Hong Kong (P.C.) ([1970] A.C. 1136)*, the Privy Council had to decide on the limits to the legislative powers of the legislative assembly of Hong Kong, called the "Legislative Council". The legislative jurisdiction of the colonial legislature is subject to imperial laws. The five members of the Judicial Committee were divided on the issue of the admissibility in law of a motion for an injunction. For purposes of the debate, it was admitted that the Legislative Council of Hong Kong had adopted an invalid law. The judges of the majority nevertheless declared that the recourse of injunction was inadmissible, because the law, which affected private interests, had not yet been assented to. This did not prevent Lord Diplock, speaking for the majority, to state that if the illegal acts of a legislature which possesses limited powers would lead to a result for which no sanctions could be obtained, the courts may intervene immediately in order to avoid the occurrence of such a result. He stated the following (p. 1157):

> "*The immunity from control by the courts, which is enjoyed by members of a legislative assembly while exercising their deliberative functions is founded on necessity. The question of the extent of the immunity which is necessary raises a conflict of public policy between the desirability of freedom of deliberation in the legislature and the observance by its members of the rule of law of which the courts are the guardians. If there will be no remedy when the legislative process is complete and the unlawful conduct in the course of the legislative process will then have achieved its object, the argument founded on necessity in their Lordships' view leads to the conclusion that there must be a remedy available in a court of justice before the result has been achieved which*

was intended to be prevented by the law from which a legislature which is not fully sovereign derives its powers."

The Plaintiff has requested that we issue a series of injunctions against the Defendants and the Government of Québec, as well as certain injunctions addressed to the Directeur général des élections. The Court can certainly not paralyse the workings of the National Assembly, nor prohibit it from debating the question. This would violate parliamentary privilege. In fact, it is better that the public debate be carried out in an informed manner.

As for prohibiting the use of public funds in the promotion of the Government's constitutional project, no injunction can be issued, since no legislative provision which deals with these expenses, which are incurred in the name of the Crown, has been brought to our attention.

Moreover, the Court has taken judicial notice that neither the Official Opposition of Québec, nor the federal Government, intends to attempt to interfere with the holding of the referendum. The issuance of an injunction against the holding of the referendum would risk creating greater harm than the harm that is sought to be prevented.

Furthermore, a declaratory judgment may have an effect which is just as effective, if not more effective, than an injunction. In fact, for several reasons, it is the remedy favoured by the courts in constitutional matters. A declaration does not interfere with the workings of the executive branch or the legislative branch. It does not open the door to enforcement procedures which may appear undesirable. On the contrary, it enables the government to try to find a way to satisfy the judicial declaration, which helps in maintaining the balance between our democratic institutions.

In addition, the declaratory remedy is better suited to preventive justice. All of these principles were set forth by Kent Roach, an attorney of the Bar of Ontario, in his work entitled "Constitutional Remedies in Canada" (Canada Law Book Inc., 1994).

CONCLUSIONS

In order to prevent the Plaintiff's recourse from becoming entirely useless at the time of the final judgment, the only declaration which appears to us to be a useful remedy is to state, as the Plaintiff has requested, that any bill which reiterates the provisions of the agreement ratified and signed on June 12, 1995 by Messrs. Jacques Parizeau, Lucien Bouchard and Mario Dumont, whose purpose is to grant the National Assembly of Québec the capacity or the power to declare the sovereignty of Quebec, without being obliged to follow the amending procedure provided for in the Constitution of Canada, constitutes a serious threat to the rights and freedoms of the Plaintiff as guaranteed by the Canadian Charter of Rights and Freedoms, in particular, by Sections 2, 3, 6, 7, 15 and 24(1).

Given that the bill entitled An Act respecting the future of Québec is included in this request, it is appropriate to adapt this declaration by specifically referring to this bill. Any other declaratory judgment would risk altering the nature of the issue before us.

Given the circumstances, the ruling will not target the Directeur général des élections who appeared through his attorneys and who indicated that he derives his powers directly from the National Assembly and not from the Government.

FOR THESE REASONS, THE COURT: –

DECLARES that Bill 1, entitled AN ACT RESPECTING THE FUTURE OF QUÉBEC, introduced by Premier Jacques Parizeau to the National Assembly on September 7, 1995, whose purpose is to grant the National Assembly the power to declare that Québec is a sovereign country, without being obliged to follow the amending process provided for in Part v of the Constitution Act, 1982, constitutes a serious threat to the rights and freedoms of the Plaintiff as guaranteed by the Canadian Charter of Rights and Freedoms, in particular, by Sections 2, 3, 6, 7, 15 and 24(1);

THE WHOLE with costs against the Defendants Bégin and Parizeau, in their respective capacities, but without costs against the Defendant Côté, in his capacity.

[signed] Robert Lesage
JUDGE OF THE SUPERIOR COURT

(57)   Me Guy Bertrand
(57)   Me Jean-François Bertrand
Attorneys for the Plaintiff

(134)   Me Jean-Yves Bernard
(134)   Me Claude Bouchard
(134)   Me Réal A. Forest
Attorneys for the Honorable
Paul Bégin and Jacques Parizeau

(4)   Me Pierre Giroux
(4)   Me Stéphane Rochette
Attorneys for Me Pierre-F. Côté

RICHMOND PUBLIC LIBRARY
3 1290 00723 5773

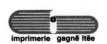
imprimerie gagné ltée

PRINTED IN CANADA